CAREER PLANNING
FOR TEENS

Discover The Proven Path to Finding a
Successful Career That's Right for You!

SETH HICKS

TABLE OF CONTENTS

INTRODUCTION

As you enter or continue your teenage years, your life as an adult may seem extremely far away, but you'll be surprised at how quickly time passes. Before you know it, you'll be ready to embark on your career — that is, if you've planned for one.

It might not seem practical to worry about a career when you're 14 or 15 years old. However, this is actually the perfect time to begin exploring career paths and setting yourself up for the journey you'll take toward your adult occupation. The world and its options are open to you, and a plan can get you where you want to go.

This guide will show you how to start thinking about the careers you might want in the future, help you narrow down your options, and create a roadmap to achieve your career-related goals. While there's more than one way to end up in a career you love, planning ahead is the most reliable strategy for teens who want their job to also be their passion.

ASSESSMENT

Some people know from an early age exactly what they want to be when they grow up, and their goals never waver. If you're someone who has always wanted to have a career as a veterinarian, astronaut, or teacher, you might be tempted to skip the assessment section of this guide. After all, you know what you want; you just need to learn how to get there.

However, the assessment is a critical component of career planning, even if you think you know what you want your career to be. Assessing your identity, strengths, and the types of careers that offer you the best odds of success will help you understand your motivations and aspirations. What exactly do you want out of life? Why do you want it? Clarifying these questions can help refine your career plan and may even open up new possibilities that you haven't yet considered.

So, whether you already have your heart set on a career or you don't have a clue, assessment is the first step toward creating the roadmap to achieving your goals.

QUESTION YOURSELF

Until you really understand yourself, you won't be able to choose a career path. You have to take the time to figure out what makes you tick. So, the initial stop on your career roadmap is to question yourself. While you don't have to write down your answers to these questions, doing so will help solidify them in your mind as you continue down the path toward career preparation. If you're not a writer, consider recording your responses to these questions to revisit later.

Interests

Certainly, the activities you already enjoy doing can give you clues about what you might enjoy doing as a job. Since the goal of career planning is to help you progress toward a satisfying and fulfilling career, using your interests as a guide is an excellent place to start. Ask yourself the following questions to pinpoint your interests:

- What are my hobbies?
- How do I spend most of my free time?
- Do I enjoy spending more time indoors or outdoors?
- Do I prefer working with people, animals, books, or data?
- What activities would I miss the most if they were no longer available to me?

Talents

Everyone is good at something, and you are no exception. Usually, by the time you get into middle school or high school, some talents have become apparent, but there are also others that you haven't yet explored. Many times, your talents align with your interests but not always. You can be talented at something you don't really enjoy doing, which is why you need to separate the two subjects when you're questioning yourself. To determine your talents, ask yourself these questions:

- What are the classes I do well in?
- Which ones seem easy?
- What awards have I received, and what are they for?
- What are my most successful projects? Which ones make me the proudest?
- What do other people tell me I'm good at?
- What could I practice over and over again without getting bored?

Values

Identifying your values and what's most important to you can provide insight into a career path that will be fulfilling and meaningful. Our values are often shaped by our parents and what they care about, but this isn't always the case, particularly if you've been impacted by different experiences and events. For instance, you might value social justice more than your parents because you live in a world where that issue has been thrust to the forefront of society. If so, you might be well-suited for a career with a nonprofit organization or a company that uses its influence to fight injustice.

Everyone has intrinsic values that motivate them throughout their daily lives. If you choose a job that doesn't align with your values, you're probably not going to be happy there, and success may be unachievable. Even if you do succeed, it might feel hollow or unsatisfying to you. Some common intrinsic values you may have include:

- Financial security
- Benefits
- Work-life balance
- Power
- Commitment
- Contribution
- Independence
- Honesty
- Equality
- Responsibility
- Respect
- Status
- Achievement
- Competition
- Loyalty
- Individualism
- Recognition
- Leadership
- Support
- Learning
- Structure
- Predictability
- Quality
- Autonomy
- Individualism

- Cooperation

There are many more values that could be motivating for you when you consider the type of career you want, but you'll need to really think about situations in which you have thrived in the past to help identify your own values. For example, some people thrive on group work in school, whereas others succeed more when they work on their own. If you fall into the latter group and you get a job that requires significant collaboration, you probably won't be content with your work.

At this point, you can list all the values you can think of that are important to you. You don't have to limit yourself to one or two of them, but later, you'll want to prioritize your list. The longer your list of values is, the more difficult it may be to find a career that meets all of them.

Dreams

Your dreams can clue you in on what you want to do as a career. They can serve as the ultimate long-term goals for your life's work and provide the framework to establish the smaller goals to reach your dreams. You might have several dreams, and that's perfectly fine. You can start with them and narrow your options down as you combine the other factors listed here to choose the dream you want to chase.

At this point, your dreams can be a bit vague. Your dream might be that you want to see your artwork in a gallery someday. Eventually, you'll get more specific when you start setting goals, but for now, write down every dream you've ever had related to what you want to achieve in your life. These questions will help guide you forward.

- Is there an award I want to receive someday (e.g., MVP of a professional sports league, Pulitzer Prize for Fiction, Oscar for Best Actress, etc.)?
- What is the highest level I can reach in my field of interest or sport?
- What do I want to own (e.g., a mansion, a specific sports car, etc.)?
- Where do I want to live (e.g., on a beach, in Italy, on an island, etc.)?
- Do I want to be famous? If so, for what?
- Do I want to change people's lives? If so, how?

Geography

If you already have your heart set on a particular career, that might dictate where you live; if you haven't yet chosen your career path, knowing your geographical preferences can have an impact on which careers are available to you.

For instance, if you decide you want to live on a rural farm in Kansas, you won't have very many opportunities to be a marine biologist. Living in a town in Vermont is not going to be conducive to becoming a movie star. Not to say that it isn't possible to be whatever you want, wherever you live, but it becomes much more challenging if you don't consider your geography at the same time you're considering your career. Although there are more options for remote work than ever before, some jobs still require applicants to attend interviews and work in person, so thinking about the type of place or actual city where you want to live is important.

Begin with some general questions about your preferred living style.

- Do you like hot or cold weather?
- Do you prefer city or rural life?
- Would you rather be near the beach or the mountains?
- Do you have any specific health concerns that would require living in a specific climate?
- Is being near family important to you?
- Would you like to experience living abroad?
- These types of questions can narrow down your geographical options.

Lifestyle

Geography and lifestyle often go hand in hand. People who love the nightlife and enjoy having numerous entertainment options probably aren't going to like living in an extremely rural location. Those who want to surf every weekend won't be able to do what they love if they live in the mountains. But more than that, your desired lifestyle can influence the career you choose. The aforementioned weekend surfer will want a career that ensures they have most weekends available to hit the waves. A retail manager isn't likely to have weekends off, so the surfer would steer themselves away from that type of career.

Other lifestyle factors that may impact your career include:

- Whether you want to have children or stay single
- Whether you're a night owl or early bird
- Whether you want to travel for your work or stay in one place

- Whether you want to make a lot of money or are satisfied with sufficient money to live comfortably.

Of course, some careers can accommodate different lifestyles, but if you're looking to become extremely wealthy, for example, there are some careers that are automatically ruled out. Asking yourself some questions like these will pare down your options based on the type of life you want.

Prioritize

The next step toward identifying a career is to take the work you did in questioning yourself and then prioritize your answers. This means you'll want to rank your answers to the questions from most important to least important to give you a better idea of what to look for in a career.

Rank your answers by section first (i.e., rank all your interests, then your talents, etc.), then decide if it's more important for you to have the lifestyle or the geography you want. This doesn't mean you won't get both eventually, but you may need to choose one or the other at some point. Knowing which you prefer now will provide insight into the choice you have to make later.

Since there are so many values that can come into play when choosing a career, you may need to start whittling them down by grouping your list of values into three categories: essential values, important values, and nice-to-have values. Don't think too long about any one value because it's best to use your instinct to rank them. When you start thinking about them too hard, you may override your original choice by allowing what other people value to influence your decision.

Start with the first two values on your list, and ask yourself which one you would choose if you could only pick one. That's your priority. Take the "winner" of the first two and do the same thing with that one and the third value on your list. Continue with that method until you have an ultimate "winner."

When you're finished prioritizing your values, interests, and talents, and you've decided whether lifestyle is more important than geography or vice versa, you'll know what characteristics to look for when you start researching careers. Keeping these items in mind will allow you to quickly exclude careers or jobs that don't match your priorities and determine which ones are a better fit for your desired path.

Familiarize Yourself with the 16 Career Clusters

Now that you've determined your top interests, talents, values, and preferences, you're ready to dive into basic career research. At this point, you need to get a general idea of what types of careers are available so that you can narrow your choices down even further.

Career clusters are groups of occupations that have similar features and usually require comparable knowledge or sets of skills. Typically, if a person is drawn to one job in a career cluster, they'll probably like another job in the same cluster. There are 16 career clusters to consider, and the answers to your questions in the previous section can help you exclude some of them right away. You might have to do further research into others before you can include or exclude them, but by familiarizing yourself with the clusters, you will have a better idea of where to start your deeper examination.

Agriculture, Food, and Natural Resources

Careers in the agriculture, food, and natural resources cluster focus on producing, processing, distributing, developing, marketing, and financing agricultural products. There are several career pathways, including those related to agribusiness, natural resources, environmental services, food processing, and other technical systems.

Examples of jobs and careers in this cluster are:

- Farmers
- Ranchers
- Animal breeders
- Environmental engineers
- Pest-control workers
- Hazardous-materials workers
- Food scientists
- Forestry and conservation workers
- Fishing and hunting workers
- Tree trimmers and pruners
- Soil and plant scientists
- Agricultural engineers
- Agricultural-equipment operators
- Farm-equipment mechanics
- Farm laborers and contractors
- Animal scientists
- Refuse and recyclable-material collectors
- Water/wastewater engineers
- Foresters
- Zoologists and wildlife biologists

Architecture and Construction

People who have jobs in the architecture and construction cluster are usually involved in designing, planning, building, managing, and maintaining structures. Most skilled trades workers like plumbers, carpenters, electricians, and HVAC technicians have careers that fall within this cluster. The career pathways in this category are construction, design/ pre-construction, maintenance, and operations. Often, people who have careers in this cluster have strong math skills, but there are some artistic occupations as well, including architects and interior designers.

Examples of jobs and careers in this cluster are:

- Architects
- Civil engineers
- Landscapers
- Plumbers
- Carpenters
- Commercial drivers
- Electrical linemen
- Elevator and escalator installers and repairers
- Civil drafters
- Boilermakers
- Highway maintenance workers
- Interior designers
- Carpet installers
- Construction laborers
- Brick masons
- Surveyors
- HVAC mechanics and installers
- Mechanical-door repairers

- Groundskeepers
- Landscape architects

Arts, Audio/Visual Technology, and Communications

Many creative jobs and careers fall under the arts, audio/visual technology, and communications cluster. These careers involve writing, designing, producing, exhibiting, performing, and publishing various media content. Performing arts, graphic design, entertainment, and journalism jobs all fall under this category, making it one of the best options for people who want to act, sing, write, or design for a living. The career pathways under this cluster are audio and visual technology and film, journalism and broadcasting, performing arts, printing technology, telecommunications, and visual arts.

Examples of jobs and careers in this cluster are:

- Audio and visual technicians
- Camera operators
- Editors
- Actors
- Dancers
- Costumers
- Musicians
- Singers
- Producers
- Directors
- Desktop publishers
- Proofreaders
- Copywriters
- Lighting technicians

- Reporters and journalists
- Photographers
- Technical writers
- Writers and authors
- Printing press operators

Business Management and Administration

Jobs and careers in the business management and administration career cluster are related to planning, directing, organizing, and evaluating business functions. Many common entry-level jobs like secretaries, receptionists, typists, and customer service representatives are included in this cluster, but it also contains high-powered positions like CEO, CFO, CIO, President, Vice President, and other executive office jobs. Career pathways that fall under this category are administrative support, general management, business information management, operations management, and human resources management.

Examples of jobs and careers in this cluster are:

- Accounting clerks
- Customer service representatives
- Secretaries
- Data entry workers
- Mail clerks
- Meter readers
- Payroll clerks
- Mail carriers
- Computer and information systems managers
- CEOs, CIOs, CFOs, and compliance managers
- Investment-fund managers

- Supply chain managers
- Human resource managers
- Fundraisers
- Energy auditors
- Purchasing managers
- Correspondence clerks
- Office clerks
- Payroll clerks
- Switchboard operators

Education and Training

The most obvious profession that falls under the education and training cluster is teacher, but there are many others that are included as well. All jobs and careers are involved in teaching and learning support but in more capacities than solely classroom experiences. There are three career pathways in this category: administration and administrative support, professional support services, and teaching and training.

Examples of jobs and careers in this cluster are:

- Teachers
- Professors
- Curators
- Counselors (educational, career)
- Instructional coordinators
- Principals
- Assistant principals
- Archivists
- Librarians

- Interpreters
- Coaches
- Scouts
- Tutors
- Translators
- Museum technicians
- Substitute teachers
- Special education teaching assistants
- Career counselors
- Childcare administrators
- Fitness and wellness coordinators

Finance

The finance cluster includes jobs and careers that deal with money matters, including managing and planning finances and investments. People who work at banks and insurance companies can fall into this category, and their positions typically work closely with the business management and administration cluster. Career pathways in this category are accounting, banking services, business finance, insurance, securities, and investments. People who enter into careers in finance often excel at math and are analytical in nature.

Examples of jobs and careers in this cluster are:

- Accountants
- Bank tellers
- Auditors
- Financial managers
- Tax preparers
- Treasurers and controllers

- Actuaries
- Claims adjusters
- Insurance claims and policy-processing clerks
- Insurance agents
- Insurance underwriters
- Brokerage clerks
- Personal finance advisors
- Financial risk specialists
- Loan officers
- Credit authorizers
- Budget analysts
- Insurance underwriters
- Fraud examiners and investigators
- Financial risk specialists

Government and Public Administration

Government and public administration careers are often highly desirable because of the benefits that are attached. These jobs and careers are involved with planning and performing government functions at the federal, state, and local levels, including governance, regulation, national security, and law-enforcement operations. Career paths that fall under the government and public administration cluster are foreign service, governance, national security, planning, public management and administration, regulation, and revenue and taxation.

Examples of jobs and careers in this cluster are:

- Foreign ambassadors
- Aviation inspectors
- Coroners

- Elected officials
- Legislators
- Air crews
- Military members
- Transportation-security screeners
- Urban and regional planners
- Court, municipal, and license clerks
- Emergency management directors
- Postmasters and mail superintendents
- Occupational health and safety specialists
- Real estate appraisers
- Tax examiners and IRS agents
- Transportation inspectors
- Urban and regional planners
- Financial examiners
- Government program eligibility interviewers

Health Science

Careers in the health-science cluster are centered on planning, managing, and providing health services. Doctors, nurses, and therapists are common professions in this category, but there are many types of doctors, nurses, and therapists that make this one of the larger career clusters of the 16. Career paths in this sector include biotechnology research and development, diagnostic services, health informatics, support services, and therapeutic services. People who work in health science fields usually have a strong interest in science.

Examples of jobs and careers in this cluster are:

- Bioengineers
- Sonographers
- Epidemiologists
- MRI technicians
- Surgical assistants
- Medical transcriptionists
- Medical records specialists
- Orderlies
- Pharmacy technicians
- Physicians
- Nurses
- Dentists
- Pharmacists
- Optometrists
- Psychiatrists
- Surgeons
- Sports medicine physicians
- Veterinarians
- Nutritionists
- Midwives

Hospitality and Tourism

The hospitality and tourism cluster covers jobs and careers involved in the management, marketing, and operations of hotels, restaurants, attractions, travel services, and recreational events. Restaurant wait staff make up a large portion of this category, but there are literally hundreds of jobs that fall into this cluster. Career paths in hospitality and tourism include lodging; recreation, amusement, and attractions; restaurants and food/beverage services; and travel and tourism. While many people get their first jobs in hospitality and tourism, there are long-term careers available at high levels as well.

Examples of jobs and careers in this cluster are:

- Concierges
- Hotel, motel, and resort desk clerks
- Lodging managers
- Maids and housekeeping cleaners
- Animal trainers
- Amusement park attendants
- Gambling dealers, managers, and attendants
- Sports officials (referees, umpires, etc.)
- Ushers and ticket takers
- Bakers
- Chefs
- Food-preparation workers
- Hosts and hostesses
- Servers
- Bartenders
- Travel agents
- Tour guides
- Film projectionists
- Dishwashers
- Baristas

Human Services

People who work in the human services fields are involved with mental health, counseling, personal care, and consumer services. While this cluster includes professions like social workers and psychologists, it also encompasses careers in hairdressing and cosmetology. Career paths in human services fall within the categories of consumer services, counseling and mental health, early childhood development, family and community services, and personal care.

Examples of jobs and careers in this cluster are:

- Credit counselors
- Loan officers
- Psychologists
- Marriage and family therapists
- Substance abuse counselors
- Childcare workers
- Nannies
- Social workers
- Clergy members
- Barbers
- Funeral home operators
- Fitness instructors
- Hairdressers
- Manicurists
- Dog walkers
- Personal care aides
- Massage therapists
- Laundry and dry-cleaning workers
- Tailors and dressmakers
- School psychologists

Information Technology

This career cluster contains jobs that are concerned with the design, development, management, support, and maintenance of computer systems. This is a highly popular career category because of the many opportunities to work with rapidly evolving technology. People who work in these fields often receive continuous education and training to stay on top of the advances in technology. Career paths in the information technology cluster include information support and services, network systems, programming and software development, and web and digital communications.

Examples of jobs and careers in this cluster are:

- Computer systems engineers
- Business intelligence analysts
- Database architects
- Document-management specialists
- Video game designers
- Web administrators
- Database administrators
- Computer network architects
- Computer programmers
- Software developers
- Web developers
- Web and digital interface designers
- Information security analysts
- Search marketing specialists
- Telecommunications-engineering specialists
- Data-warehousing specialists
- Software quality assurance analysts and testers

- Health informatics specialists
- Network and computer systems administrators
- Computer user support specialists

Law, Public Safety, Corrections, and Security

Having a career in the law, public safety, corrections, and security cluster means you'll be involved in providing protection, public safety, and legal services to your community. Common professions in these fields include law enforcement officers, lawyers, and security guards, but within each of those general professions, there are many types of specialties (e.g., criminal lawyer) and support positions that are necessary for operations. Career paths in this category are based in correctional services, emergency and fire management, law enforcement, legal services, and security and protective services.

Examples of jobs and careers in this cluster are:

- Correctional officers
- Probation officers
- Emergency medical technicians
- Firefighters
- Paramedics
- Public safety telecommunications operators
- Animal control workers
- Customs and border patrol officers
- Fish and game wardens
- Forensic services technicians
- Police officers
- Private detectives
- Lawyers

- Judges
- Paralegals
- Bailiffs
- Lifeguards
- Ski patrol officers
- Security guards
- Crossing guards

Manufacturing

The manufacturing career cluster includes jobs that involve planning, processing, and managing materials. Workers in these fields often use their hands or specialty equipment to create products. Production and maintenance jobs for various machines are also prevalent in this sector. Career paths include health, safety, and environmental assurance; logistics and inventory control; maintenance, installation, and repair; manufacturing process development; and quality assurance.

Examples of jobs and careers in this cluster are:

- Environmental compliance officers
- Audio/visual equipment installers and repairers
- Home appliance repairers
- Industrial machinery mechanics
- Medical equipment repairers
- Locksmiths
- Musical instrument repairers and tuners
- Watch and clock repairers
- Aerospace engineering technicians
- Mechanical drafters
- Butchers and meat cutters

- Etchers and engravers
- Factory machine operators
- Plant technicians
- Machinists
- Inspectors
- Sorters
- Tool and die makers
- Team assemblers
- Sewing machine operators

Marketing

People who work in marketing are involved in planning, managing, and performing sales activities in all other clusters. Nearly all businesses need some sort of marketing materials or activities to promote their products or services. Marketing and sales professionals create commercials, ads, and other marketing materials to help companies make sales. Career paths in marketing include communications, management, research, merchandising, and professional sales.

Examples of jobs and careers in this cluster are:

- Public relations specialists
- Fundraising managers
- Marketing managers
- Advertising and promotions managers
- Sales managers
- Market research analysts
- Merchandise displayers and window trimmers
- Models

- Wholesale and retail buyers
- Advertising sales agents
- Cashiers
- Counter and rental clerks
- Parts salespersons
- Real estate brokers and sales agents
- Retail salespersons
- Telemarketers
- Sales representatives
- First-line supervisors of retail and nonretail sales workers
- Community association managers
- Demonstrators and product promoters

Science, Technology, Engineering, and Mathematics

Some of the most highly educated individuals have careers in this cluster, and you should have a strong interest in science and math to pursue a career in these fields. While not all of them require strong math and science skills, most do. STEM classes throughout middle school and high school will best prepare you for the career paths associated with this cluster, which are engineering and technology, science, and mathematics. Since quite a bit of education is required for many of these careers, you should also be passionate about continued learning.

Examples of jobs and careers in this cluster are:

- Aerospace engineers
- Chemical engineers
- Mining safety engineers

- Computer hardware engineers
- Mechanical engineers
- Petroleum engineers
- Industrial engineers
- Fuel cell engineers
- Nuclear engineers
- Astronomers
- Anthropologists
- Archaeologists
- Biochemists
- Bioinformatics scientists
- Data scientists
- Research assistants
- Radio frequency identification device (RFID) specialists
- Naval architects
- Ergonomists
- Atmospheric and space scientists

Transportation, Distribution, and Logistics

The careers in the transportation, distribution, and logistics category help get products, materials, and people from point A to point B by air, road, pipeline, water, or rail. Related support services such as transportation-infrastructure planning, equipment maintenance, facility maintenance, and logistics services are also included in this cluster. Career paths for this category are facility and mobile-equipment maintenance; health, safety, and environmental management; logistics planning and management services; sales and service; transportation operations;

transportation management and regulation; and warehousing and distribution center operations.

Examples of jobs and careers in this cluster are:

- Aircraft mechanics and service technicians
- Automotive mechanics
- Bicycle repairers
- Rail car repairers
- Signal and track-switch repairers
- Tire repairers and changers
- Dispatchers
- Logisticians
- Billing and posting clerks
- Cargo and freight agents
- Freight forwarders
- Parking attendants
- Bus drivers
- Pilots
- Taxi drivers
- Flight attendants
- Shuttle drivers
- Air traffic controllers
- Delivery drivers
- Hand packaging goods

Take Formal Career Assessments

The good news is that you don't have to figure out what your future career looks like on your own. There are plenty of resources available to help you determine various factors that have been linked with career success and satisfaction.

Taking a good long look at yourself by asking the aforementioned questions and familiarizing yourself with the 16 career clusters is an excellent start, but now you're ready to use some of the formal career assessments to add more information to your arsenal as you plan for your career. There are many free career assessments you can take and even more that you can pay for. However, the goal here is to get some expert opinions based on scientific analysis about the careers that would likely suit you best in terms of your personality, work preferences, aptitudes, and more.

The career assessments listed and described below are some of the most prominent and well-regarded assessments available today. They have a long track record of matching respondents with careers and jobs that align with assessment results.

It is recommended that you take at least one assessment, but taking more won't hurt. In fact, the more assessments you take, the more information you'll have about yourself and the factors that will help you find a career you'll succeed in and enjoy. Don't worry if you get conflicting information from two or more assessments. They aren't designed to tell you which job you should have. They are only meant to suggest ideas for careers that you may not have considered based on your answers.

Conflicting results could arise from various outside influences on the day you take the assessment or from the way in which the questions are asked. Just keep in mind that these assessments aren't making your career decision for you. They are simply providing ideas. You aren't going to use these results in isolation, so don't stress over taking the assessments. They are one piece of the puzzle and not the entire solution. Still, they can offer valuable insight into your career preferences.

Personality and Aptitude Tests

The Myers-Briggs test is probably the most well-known career-assessment tool that's currently available. The company describes its assessment as a "personality inventory" that seeks to make sense of people's behaviors and decisions. You will be asked to make choices based on your preferences in approximately 90 scenarios. For example, you might be asked a question like, "When the phone rings, do you hasten to answer it or hope someone else will answer?"

Even though some questions might not seem career related, the assessment actually gathers information about various aspects of all types of jobs that can come into play when you're an employee. If, for instance, you select that you "hope someone else will answer" when the phone rings, you may not be well-suited for a job requiring phone work. Of course, none of the results are based on a single answer to a single question, so again, don't get hung up on how you're answering. Go with your instinct and the results will be accurate.

The Myers-Briggs assessment has been in use for more than 40 years, giving people insight into their own preferences and choices based on 16 personality types. This test will not give you career options based on your answers, but knowing your personality type will help you find careers that allow your personality to shine. When you learn your Myers-Briggs personality type, you'll have more information to help you narrow down your career choices. For instance, if your personality comes back as an ISFJ (introvert, sensor, feeler, judger), you can search for "jobs that are good for ISFJ" and get specific results.

Holland Code Career Aptitude Test

This assessment is more focused on career and vocational choices than the Myers-Briggs, which can be used for numerous applications in both personal and professional circumstances. The Holland Code Career Aptitude Test consists of 48 to 72 sample tasks. It will ask you to rate how much you would enjoy doing each based on a scale of one to five, with one being dislike, two being slightly dislike, three being neither like nor dislike, four being slightly enjoy, and five being enjoy. The test only takes about 10 minutes to complete, making it significantly shorter than the Myers-Briggs. The results will indicate your suitability for six different occupational categories: Realistic, Investigative, Artistic, Social, Enterprising, and Conventional.

You will receive a three-letter code that can be used to match your personality to various work environments. For instance, if you receive the code S.E.C., you are considered Social, Enterprising, and Conventional, which means you would be well-suited for a career that follows traditional rules and is focused on interacting with and helping others. As with the Myers-Briggs assessment, you can take your three-letter code and search for careers that align with the associated personality traits in those categories.

The Holland Code Career Aptitude Test can be taken online for free, or you can take a paid version with more questions. It's ideal for people who don't want to spend a lot of time on assessments but still want to have an idea of where to start their career search.

Motivational Appraisal of Personal Potential (MAPP) Aptitude Test

The Motivational Appraisal of Personal Potential, or MAPP assessment, is considered the most comprehensive career assessment available because it not only assesses your personality but also matches the results to actual careers and jobs that you'll likely succeed in and enjoy. It has been in use for more than 20 years. It's used primarily for people who are initially searching for a career and those who are transitioning from one career to another. It only takes a little over 20 minutes to get your results, which are immediately delivered to you based on your answers to 71 questions.

On the assessment, you will be given three statements and asked to identify which one you like the most and which one you like the least. The third statement will be left blank. For example, you might be given the following three statements:

- Teach art at an elementary or high school
- Teach science at a high school or college
- Coach athletics at a high school or college

You would choose the one that appeals to you the most and the one that appeals to you the least while leaving the third blank. As with the other assessments listed here, you shouldn't take too long to think about each question because your instincts usually provide the most accurate response.

The MAPP assessment does require a fee, so it's not the most economical assessment out there. For the base price of $89.95, you will be able to take the assessment, receive your top 20 general career matches, and have the ability to self-match to 50 other careers. At this point, it's recommended that you choose only the base level because the higher levels may give you too many career choices to be helpful.

Keirsey Temperament Aptitude Sorter

Temperament is part of your personality, but it's not the same thing as your personality. Your temperament is generally inherited, while your personality is developed on top of your temperament. Essentially, your temperament is your emotional response to outside influences and is often instinctual in nature. While temperament can be shaped to some degree, it's set early in life (in fact, as early as birth), whereas personality is developed over many years based on a wide variety of factors.

The Keirsey Temperament Aptitude Sorter uses answers to 70 questions to place you in one of four temperament types: Artisan, Guardian, Rational, and Idealist. Within these temperament types, your responses will further sort you into one of an additional four character types:

- Artisan: Promoter, Crafter, Performer, Composer
- Guardian: Supervisor, Inspector, Provider, Protector
- Rational: Field Marshal, Mastermind, Inventor, Architect
- Idealist: Teacher, Counselor, Champion, Healer

While this assessment is closely linked to the Myers-Briggs assessment (and you can actually use the Myers-Briggs results to place you in a temperament category without taking the assessment), there are differences between the two that are helpful in career selection. Understanding your temperament can provide insight into how you interact with other people and your environment. In other words, knowing your temperament gives you deeper knowledge about which careers are right for you.

The Keirsey Temperament Aptitude Sorter is free to take, but the company does charge for a report on your results. The Careers Report, which is the one recommended for first-time career searchers, is $18.71. There are various other reports you can purchase as well to see how your results affect various areas of your life, such as leadership, romance, and learning.

Career Explorer Career Test

The Career Explorer Career Test purports to combine the best features of all the other listed career assessments, and it's free to take. As with other assessments, you'll answer a series of questions to determine your "personality archetype," which will tell you how you're unique and why certain careers may better suit you than others.

The assessment is made up of five modules: the Welcome Assessment, the History & Goals Assessment, the Workplace Assessment, the Interests Assessment, and the Personality Assessment. The entire test is designed to take no longer than 30 minutes. You can opt to take two additional models, the Personality Refinement Assessment and the Interests Refinement Assessment, which will take an extra 16 minutes.

One aspect that makes this assessment different from others is that it also takes into account your previous work experience and salary history to suggest careers that would be good extensions of the types of work you've already done. As a first-time career searcher, you might not have any experience to offer, but if you do, this assessment will use it to provide more detailed results.

By taking the free assessment, you will receive:

- A list of twelve career matches based on your answers to the questions in each module
- A list of characteristics that are unique to your personality that you can combine with the results from other assessments
- A Personality Report that provides insight on how your traits could combine to fit into certain job roles
- A Trait Report that categorizes you into six areas of interest.

More detailed reports are available for a fee.

CONVERSATION

Now that you've taken stock of your personal attributes and conducted preliminary research on the 16 career clusters, you're ready to move onto the next stage of career planning. At this stage, you'll need to have a series of conversations with the adults in your life who spend the most time around you and know you best. As with the assessments, the conversations you have won't tell you what career you should pursue. Instead, you'll gather valuable information about what traits and qualities others observe in you that could be clues to your best career options.

Remember that the adults in your life want to see you succeed. They will give you insights that they truly believe are in your best interests. Even if you don't agree with what they have to say, keep an open mind. You never know when something they say might trigger your interest in a new career direction.

Parents

Teenagers aren't known for wanting to have conversations with their parents, but when it comes to your career, this is one conversation you need to have. Your parents, guardians, family members, or teachers may know you best from your earliest moments, so they have information about your interests and skills that no one else does. Some people begin showing an aptitude or talent for a potential career path from the time they are toddlers. While this isn't the norm, there are still hints to the type of person you are and the things you enjoy doing.

Keep in mind that a conversation isn't a one-way dialogue from them to you or you to them. You should bring up what you discovered about yourself in the assessment phase of your research and ask them which parts they agree or disagree with. This exercise might bring up something they remember from your childhood that aligns with a result you received. For instance, you may have cared for a creature you found in the back yard one time, which confirms your aptitude for working with animals. You parents have so many memories of you that sometimes it takes a conversation like this to bring some of them to the forefront.

It's very common for kids to follow in their parents' footsteps in terms of career. They are influenced from an early age by the things they see their parents doing, and because parents are the strongest role models in kids' lives, children frequently idolize their professions. Usually, though, parents are open to any career that will be fulfilling to you as an individual, whether that's the same career they have or a completely unrelated one.

If you're considering going into the same career as one of your parents, ask them questions about their daily duties, what they like and dislike about their jobs, and whether they think you are well-suited for the work that's required. You are not your parents, so you might not have the same personality that allowed them to succeed in their professions. That's okay. You have plenty of options that can take you wherever you want to go.

Some parents might already have a career in mind for you and may have been directing you toward that career all your life. Now is the time to assess that career and determine if it's right for you. You may need to have a hard conversation with your parents about your career preferences and goals, but as long as you've done the assessment work, you'll have data to back up your choices. If you aren't ready to have this type of discussion with your parents, you can simply tell them that their career suggestion is one of many you're considering at this time.

Guidance Counselor

Your guidance counselor at school is one of the best resources you have at your disposal when it comes to career planning. They are trained to help students determine their path in life after high school, whether that involves going to college, getting vocational training, or going directly to work. They are a free resource that you should definitely use to your advantage.

In some schools, the guidance counselor will have a set curriculum that they will deliver to students to help them choose their careers. Often, this will involve many of the assessments listed in this book and other tools that can offer insight into your skills, interests, and aptitudes. Your counselor might also set aside time to meet with each student to have in-depth conversations about your assessment results and career goals. This is the perfect opportunity to bring up your own research and ask them to give you their honest opinions.

If your counselor doesn't have a set curriculum for career planning, you will need to be more proactive about seeking their assistance. Schedule an appointment with your counselor, and tell them you have some questions about your career-planning strategy. Before your meeting day, ask yourself these questions:

- What do I want to get out of this meeting with my counselor?

- What parts of career planning do I want assistance with?
- How do I think my counselor can help me with my career-planning strategy?

Knowing the answers to these questions will keep your meeting focused so that you can spend most of the time you have scheduled talking about the heart of the matter. You'll be able to stay on track during the discussion instead of wandering outside of what you really need from your counselor.

You should also have a list of questions you want your counselor to answer. They may not be prepared to answer all those questions during your meeting, but you can ask to leave the questions with them so that they can really put a lot of thought into their responses. You may also need to meet with your counselor several times as you plan for your career and your path becomes more certain. In that case, the first set of questions will be for your initial meeting, and the second set will be for subsequent meetings.

Questions for your first meeting:

- What do you see as my strengths?
- What do you see as my weaknesses?
- What do you recommend I do to improve my weaknesses?
- What careers do you know of that are aligned with my strengths?
- What courses should I take to be ready for post-secondary education of any kind (college, junior college, specialty programs, apprenticeships, internships, etc.)?
- What kinds of grades do colleges require?
- What information do you have to help me in my career exploration?

- Are there any career fairs planned in the school's area?
- Are there any career speakers planned for our school?

Questions for subsequent meetings:

- Which Advanced Placement courses or honors courses should I take?
- How should I study for the SAT?
- Should I take the ACT as well as the SAT?
- Do you have any college brochures that specialize in my chosen career?
- What activities can I do at home to prepare for post-secondary education?
- Can you put me in touch with other people who are currently working in my chosen career?
- Can you put me in touch with other people who are attending the colleges I am considering?
- Can I see my transcripts to know where I currently stand and what I need to do to reach my goals?

Be aware that your counselor may give you advice that you don't like or agree with. Again, they are giving you their opinion based on their observations of you and your results on their assessments. You don't have to follow their advice, but the information they give you can be useful when combined with the other research you're doing. Their opinion should never be the only one you take, just as the results from one assessment shouldn't be the only results you consider for choosing a career.

Teachers

Your teachers know you better than just about anyone other than your family and friends. They work with you day in and day out to help you prepare for life after high school. This preparation includes career planning, and they should be more than happy to discuss your future plans with you. Teachers see your strengths and weaknesses every day and can give you advice on which careers would take advantage of your strengths.

If you're looking for additional resources for career planning, your teachers can help you there as well. They will be familiar with career-assessment tools, books, videos, and possibly even shadowing opportunities that they can direct you to for continued research.

While your teachers in classes you do well in are great options for career exploration, consider talking to the teachers of classes in which you struggle as well. It might be more difficult to start a conversation with these teachers, but they could have incredible insight into how you can improve your weaknesses to pursue careers in those fields. And, if you should probably avoid careers in those areas, they'll know that, too.

For those of you who already have an idea of the career you want to pursue, be sure to schedule discussions with teachers who teach related classes. For example, if you intend to be an automobile mechanic, seeking advice from your school's shop teacher would be an excellent way to learn more about potential jobs, apprenticeships, or continuing-education opportunities. If you're looking to pursue acting, your drama teacher is a readily available resource for you and can steer you toward classes, camps, and private lessons to get you on your way.

Of course, if you intend to go into teaching as a career, you can definitely get your fill of advice from any one of your teachers. They will show you the steps you need to take to become a teacher, provide a wide range of resources, and encourage you along the way.

Coaches

As with teachers, your coaches spend a lot of time with you, especially during specific seasons. Even if you're not planning to pursue a career in a sport, your coaches can still assist with career planning by talking with you about your strengths on the field or court.

Almost all sports help build skills that will translate to your career, no matter what path you choose. Skills like leadership, time management, persistence, dedication, and responsibility are part and parcel of nearly every job you'll ever hold. Coaches will help you develop these skills so that you're well-prepared to make the leap from high school to post-secondary education or a career. And because a large part of their job is to observe their athletes, they will have insights into your skills that others won't have.

If you're looking to pursue a career in a specific sport or become a coach yourself, you should seek out your coaches' advice and opinions even more frequently than otherwise. They will point you in the direction of resources that can help you achieve your dreams, including camps, schools, personal trainers, private coaches, and more. They can also help you plan your path to take your athletic ability to its highest point.

If an athletic scholarship is a possibility, talk to your coaches about how to make that happen. You might have to invite college scouts to your games or send them videos of your accomplishments in your sport. Your coaches might have to contact colleges on your behalf and even send in letters of recommendation. You will need to work with your athletic team to get your abilities in front of prospective colleges, so don't be afraid to bring this subject up early in your high school experience.

ATTEND CAREER FAIRS (PRELIMINARY)

Career fairs, also referred to as career expos or job fairs, are events that are normally designed for job-recruitment purposes. Employers are looking for potential employees, and job seekers are looking to learn more about job roles and openings at companies. Usually, there are dozens of companies represented at these fairs, and potential employees come prepared to interview or at least give their resumes to companies that spark their interest.

At this point along your career-planning journey, you're not ready to interview for jobs or even hand your resume to recruiters. After all, you're probably still in high school! Fortunately, another reason people go to career fairs is to learn about job roles that they may never have heard of before. And right now, this is your purpose for attending career fairs. Later, when you're actively searching for a position or internship, you'll attend other career fairs with a different goal in mind.

The first place to look for career fairs in your area is in your counselor's office. They constantly get materials on career fairs and other events, so they can give you the information you need to attend them. Sometimes, your school will even plan a field trip to a career fair or host one at the school as a way to expose students to careers they may not know about. Take advantage of attending career fairs that are specifically geared toward high school students because they will be more explanatory about their industry and job roles than general career fairs will be.

There are websites dedicated to posting information about career fairs, including National Career Fairs, Job Fairs Near Me, HireX, and JobFairX. You can also search event sites like Eventbrite or AllEvents by narrowing your search to career fairs in your local area. Major job-search sites such as Indeed, Monster, and SimplyHired also list career fairs on their platforms.

You don't need to attend many, but the ones you do attend should include a wide range of companies so that you can get as much information as possible about various career opportunities. Unless you're already sure of a career path, you should also steer clear of industry-specific career fairs because they won't be as insightful as those that have representatives from numerous industries.

Virtual career fairs have also become common as more events moved online during the 2020 pandemic. These are an excellent way to visit with employers that offer careers not available in your area. Local career fairs may be limited to the jobs that are prevalent in your city or county, but virtual events have no such restrictions. Many individual employers also offer virtual fairs, so include them in your online search when looking for events to attend.

Questions to Ask Employers at a Career Fair

Your first foray into career exploration at a fair might be a bit overwhelming, especially if you choose one that adults are also attending. Don't let yourself feel daunted, though. You just need to be prepared, and the best way to do that is to have a list of questions to ask employers when you're talking to them at a fair. This is known as an "informational interview," and company representatives are expecting at least some of these when they attend a job fair.

When you arrive at a booth at a career fair, you'll be met by a company representative or recruiter. You can tell them you're a student researching careers so that they know you're not looking for employment yet but that you might be in the future. They will be happy to discuss the various roles they have available and will want to answer your questions.

There will probably be many job titles at each company, so you won't be able to get specific answers for every single possible career that's available at each business. So, start by asking the recruiter to give you an example of career roles at their company. Then, choose one of the roles and ask the questions below to help you become more familiar with jobs in various industries.

- What job roles do you have at your company?
- What education is required?
- What skills are required?
- What is the salary range?
- What are the working hours?
- What benefits does your company offer?
- What does career advancement look like?
- What does a typical day look like?
- What are the biggest challenges?
- What do you specifically like about working in this industry?
- What kind of person is most successful in this industry?
- Do you offer shadowing opportunities?

o   If so, how can I contact you to set up a job shadow?

Keep in mind that the answers to these questions will be different based on which role you're talking about. Try to get answers about several careers at each job fair you attend to have a sizable sample of career information from people who actually know about each.

As you're talking to company representatives, take notes or use a recording device — with the representative's permission — so that you have their answers for later research. You won't remember everything that every representative tells you, and you'll need to be able to recall their answers later when you start looking deeper into the careers you discover.

Each representative at an in-person job fair will have literature about their company and usually their specific job opportunities. Be sure to collect any materials from companies you speak with to start a file for career research. Of course, you will find careers at these events that you have no interest in. You don't have to bring home literature for those companies and can cross those potential careers off your list. Learning more about jobs you may like or dislike is a big part of why you're exploring career fairs at this stage in the first place.

Career Fair Tips

Even though you don't intend to interview at the career fairs you attend during this phase of your career research, you should still treat the fairs like professional events. You should put your best foot forward because you never know what opportunities might present themselves when you're doing your research. Perhaps you get offered a job-shadowing opportunity that leads to an internship later. Maybe you meet someone who's already working in the job of your dreams and wants to mentor you through your career-planning process. You just never know, so take these tips to heart.

- Dress nicely (no jeans, shorts, t-shirts, tank tops, etc.).
- Professionally introduce yourself by giving your name and reason you're at the fair.
- Shake hands (if the company representative is open to it).
- Research the companies attending before you go to make sure you visit with the ones you're most interested in.
- Maintain eye contact when you're speaking.
- Speak clearly.
- Don't take more than one of the recruiter giveaways (pens, stickers, lanyards, etc.).

Remember that career fairs are very serious for both the companies and the people attending them. Respect the company representatives' time, and be aware that many attendees are trying to get hired. Be on your best behavior, and dedicate yourself to learning as much as you can while you're there.

RESEARCH SPECIFIC CAREERS

By now, you should have a nice long list of potential careers that at least spark some interest in you. You probably don't know everything about these careers, but they've been identified as jobs you will likely succeed in and will satisfy at least some part of your personal needs and wants. Of course, all jobs have their advantages and disadvantages, so now's the time to start digging into your top choices a little deeper.

Make a List

Start your deeper research by making a list of every career that the assessment phase identified as possible matches for you. Don't filter out any jobs at this time. The goal is to get the full list of every career you found during the first stage of research. There may be many, but that's okay. You're going to narrow your options down soon, but right now, you're actually going to add to the list.

Every career has related jobs that most people don't know about that could end up being the perfect opportunity for you. Most of the time, employees don't learn about these positions until they're actually working in the field, but if you take the time to identify them now, you won't have to wait before finding your ideal position, especially if it happens to be a more obscure job. During this part of your career-planning path, take some time to identify these lesser-known careers.

LinkedIn is a great way to identify job titles related to careers you've already found. Start by searching for the name of a career.

49

You'll see many job openings, companies, people, and posts pop up for that career, but as you search further down in the results, you'll start to see related job opportunities. For example, if you search *travel agent*, you can see all the openings for a travel agent. If you scroll down to people and posts, you'll start to see related careers like *manager of leisure travel, travel editor, travel consultant,* and more.

You can also do a general search in Google for unusual or unique jobs that will bring up numerous sites and articles that can provide ideas to add to your list. For instance, if you're interested in a career that centers around food, but don't want to work in a restaurant, you can search for unusual food careers and come up with jobs like *chocolate taster, honey sommelier,* or *food lawyer.*

Repeat this process for the list of careers you already have, and add the unusual careers you find that pique your interest to that list. Most articles or posts have descriptions of these obscure careers so that you can determine whether or not you think you'd enjoy them before adding them to your list. There's no need to research every single lesser-known job you find, but you want to make sure you have scoured the options before getting started on the next step.

Identify In-Demand Careers

While you can certainly have career dreams in any field, you also need to be practical. There are some careers that aren't in demand, which will make it more challenging for you to sustain a career if you choose that path. This is not to say you can't do it, and if your heart is set on a specific job that's not in demand, by all means do everything possible to make it happen. But it's also a good idea to know which careers on your list are in high demand so that you have more opportunities to succeed.

The best way to see if a job is in demand is to look at current job openings on sites like Indeed, Monster, LinkedIn, Glassdoor, and ZipRecruiter, among others. Search for each career on one or more of these sites, and see how many openings come up. If there are many, the career is in demand. If there are few, it's probably not in demand right now. This can certainly change by the time you start looking for a job yourself, but in most cases, the jobs that are in demand now will likely still be in demand a few years down the road.

Keep in mind, though, that the reverse is not always true. Jobs that aren't in demand right now could very well be in demand in 5 or 10 years, especially as technology changes and advances. To find out if a potential career will be hot when you're ready to enter the workforce, you'll have to look for projection and market-sizing articles. Search for *jobs that will be in demand in 10 years* to bring up numerous projection articles about the careers that experts believe will be needed in the future. Make a list of the jobs that are already on your list that are expected to be in demand 5 or 10 years from now, and add any that you find during your search that might be related to a career of interest or that you think could be a good match for your skills.

Filter Career Options

At this point, you should have a fairly exhaustive list of careers that are possibilities for you based on your interests, skills, assessment results, and other research. It might seem overwhelming to see so many choices, but you want to know that you've done your best to find most of the careers that you could see yourself working in.

Now, you're going to sort your list into three categories:

- Top choices
- Possibilities
- Dislikes

Remember how you prioritized your values in the assessment section? Here, you're going to do the same thing for the careers in your top choices and possibilities categories. Rank your top choices with one being the career you'd most like to pursue as of today with the last number being the career that you would cut first. Don't think too much about your choices, and go with your instincts based on everything you've learned about yourself throughout this process. This isn't a permanent decision, so don't stress over your ranking.

The careers in the possibilities category should be ranked based on demand level. This is because you will only dip into this category if you decide your top choices aren't going to work out for you once you start doing in-depth research. You've already decided they aren't exactly what you're looking for in a career, but they might be worth more scrutiny if you discover the top choices aren't what you think they are.

You can remove the careers you actively dislike from your list. Unless every career in the possibilities and top choices categories doesn't work out after deeper investigation, which is unlikely, you won't worry about your dislikes category again. If you're re-reading through them and don't want to get rid of one or more, move those to the possibilities category instead.

In-Depth Research

Starting with the career you ranked number one in the top choices category, begin researching everything you can about each career still on your list. This may be time consuming depending on how many careers are left on your list, but it's a critical step toward planning your career from here on out. You need to know the details of each career in order to make an educated decision. As long as you start this process early, before you have to make a decision about college or entering the workforce, then you'll have plenty of time to research all the careers on your list.

Set aside time each week to devote to this research. How much time you schedule will depend on how many careers you have to research, but it's recommended to spend an hour to an hour and a half each week on career planning from here on out.

To find out more about each career choice:

- Watch career-specific videos.
- Read or listen to interviews with people in those careers.
- Make a list of required education and skills.

Career-Specific Videos

You can search for career-specific videos on YouTube, but the quality will vary widely based on who made the video. Alternatively, CareerOneStop.org has put together 2-minute-or-less videos on a large number of careers organized by career cluster. These will provide you with an overview, which is a good way to introduce yourself to each.

Dr.Kit is another site that provides overview videos featuring real people discussing their careers. These are a little more in-depth than the ones on CareerOneStop but still short enough to hold your attention. KQED.org has videos for more niche careers, which might end up adding more options to your list, but that's perfectly okay, especially if it leads to your dream career!

To discover what a typical day looks like for someone in a specific career, visit Going-Pro.com, a site that offers a variety of day-in-the-life videos that show you exactly what you would be doing if you were to pursue a career in one of those fields. This website features careers in manufacturing, automotive, IT, healthcare, and construction. If you're thinking about a career in a trade, these videos will help you visualize yourself on the job.

Day at Work videos are also available on the ConnectedStudies.org website. You'll find short videos following people working throughout their day. This website is less focused on trades than Going-Pro.com, so if you're interested in careers that require a college degree or graduate degree, you'll find many of them on this website.

Many more career-related videos exist on the internet, and you can quickly fall down a rabbit hole watching video after video. It's a good idea to limit yourself to a handful of videos for each career. If video is the best way you learn, you can watch as many as you want, but if you learn better by reading or just listening, move on to the next section.

Interviews

Listening to or reading interviews with people who are already in specific careers can give you insights about jobs that you won't get through promotional videos. A great way to find these interviews is through podcasts that focus on career searches. One particular podcast that features interviews with working professionals is the Lorain County Community College Career Exploration Podcast. Even though it focuses on the college majors available at that specific school, you can hear from real people working in careers you're interested in. Recent episodes include "So You Want a Job in Healthcare," "So You Want to Combat Viruses," "So You Want to be an FBI Agent," "So You Want to be in Broadcasting," "So You Want to be an Accountant," and more. If you'd rather read about these careers, the transcripts for each episode are available for free download.

My Next Step: Career Exploration Spotlight produces podcast episodes that interview people in careers such as a food-truck owner and caterer, hair stylist, artist and creative director, designer, NASA employee, social worker, teacher, lawyer, banker, videographer, and numerous others. These podcast episodes range from just a few minutes to about 20 minutes long and provide insights into careers from the people who are living them.

You'll find both podcasts and videos of interviews with career professionals at the Career Compass Corner of the eDynamicLearning website. These are very short snippets of conversations with professionals in careers like construction management, architecture, education, filmmaking, sales-operations management, investigations, law, public service, accounting, medicine, and more. Each one is typically under three minutes.

Another resource that contains thousands of video and podcast interviews with professionals is CandidCareer.com. You'll discover interviews with a classical musician, an IT specialist, a mechanical engineer, a wealth advisor, a dental hygienist, an event planner, a journalist, a fashion merchandiser, and hundreds of others. These interviews are all between 2.5 and 5 minutes long.

Written interviews are less common but can be found by searching for interviews that focus on the specific career you're researching. For example, if you want to find a written interview with a flight attendant, you can search for *interviews with flight attendants*, and you'll get results like this great written interview from JobShadow.com. You will also come across written interviews on industry-specific sites such as this one from IBC Aviation.

List of Required Education and Skills

The next part of your career research involves determining the required education and skills for each career on your list. Most jobs will require similar "soft" skills, such as time management, flexibility, teamwork, collaboration, problem solving, and so on. You don't need to spend much time on listing those skills because they will be developed no matter which career you pursue. The skills you need to focus on are those that are specific to each career.

For example, if being a lawyer is one of your preferred career choices, you'll list items like analytical and research skills, persuasive communication, excellent written communication, interpersonal skills, public speaking, and the ability to work under pressure and tight deadlines. While some of these might appear on other lists, they are the skills that a lawyer needs to develop throughout their education and training.

When listing the required education for a career, list all post–high school degrees, certificates, licenses, and coursework necessary to fulfill the desired job role. Most careers these days already require a minimum education level of a high school diploma, and an increasing number require a bachelor's degree, which is a four-year degree from an accredited university or college. Some careers may require specialized training, as you will see with trades like plumbing or HVAC. Others require advanced education such as a master's degree or doctorate.

Some careers like becoming a teacher currently require a bachelor's degree, teaching certificate, and teaching license to become a kindergarten through high school teacher. If you want to land higher on the pay scale, you'll want to complete a master's degree as well. In a case like this, be sure to list the minimum education you need to start your career and any additional education that will allow you to advance. This will help when you plan out your career path.

Visit a Workplace or Shadow Someone Already in a Career

This step might not be feasible for every job on your initial list, but the best way to really understand what a career involves is to visit a workplace or shadow someone who's already making a living in the career you're researching. This is where connections from the job fairs you attended will come in handy. If the company representative agreed to help you shadow an employee, this is the time to call or email that representative to set it up.

Even if you're only able to visit a work site or shadow an employee for a partial day, it's still a valuable experience. Be sure to come to the job with a list of questions you have about the specific position and industry in general so that you can round out your research. This type of experience will help you learn more about the day-to-day responsibilities of someone working in that career, which is something you can best learn by observing yourself.

When you're planning a visit to a work site, find out the dress code and make sure you follow it. In some cases, it's a matter of safety (wearing steel-toed boots on a construction site), and in others, it's about professionalism (wearing a dress or suit in a law office). This is something you definitely want to ask about before you show up, along with any other logistical questions, including where you should park, who you should ask for when you arrive, and whether there are any forms to fill out beforehand, including waivers and non-disclosure agreements.

If possible, take notes during your experience, and after it's over, record your observations. You'll want to do this as soon as you can following your visit so that you don't forget anything and will be able to recall the details when you move on to the next stage of your career-planning journey.

It's also recommended that you send the person you shadowed a thank you note, either by mail or email. They took time out of their day to show you around and answer your questions, so you want to show your appreciation. This small gesture will hopefully encourage them to allow others to shadow them in the future.

Reassess Career Options

When you've finished your in-depth research, it's time to reassess your career options by regrouping them in the three categories mentioned earlier: top choices, possibilities, and dislikes. It's probable that at least some of them have moved categories, and your dislikes category has probably grown. After all, once you learn the details of a career and actually visit a work site, you're going to know about some of the disadvantages of a job that you weren't aware of before.

Hopefully, the number of careers in the top choices and possibilities sections has become smaller through research, and you'll have fewer decisions to make in the next section. If you still have quite a few careers in these two categories, you may need to conduct additional research to narrow down your choices before you move on to the next stage.

Just as you did before, rank your top choices from one — meaning the career you would most like to have — to the last. The careers in the possibilities category should be ranked on demand level. This should already be completed from the first grouping, but if any of your careers switched categories, be sure to look up their demand level before moving on.

Narrow Career Possibilities

During this phase of the process, you'll begin narrowing your top career choices and possibilities down even further. To do this, make a list of pros and cons for each career in the top choices and possibilities categories. These should be pros and cons that became apparent during your in-depth research (videos, podcasts, articles, interviews, and on-site visits). Be honest with your list because you really want to assess the careers based on their merits.

The pros and cons you put on your list should be based on your own opinions and observations. You're sure to find plenty of pros and cons about the careers on your list on the internet or from people you know, but those are other people's opinions. What might be considered a negative to one person could be a positive to another. Certainly, you can look at other people's lists, but try not to let them sway you if you don't feel the same way they do.

At this point, you may also want to have additional conversations with your parents, counselor, teachers, and coaches, especially if you've been keeping them posted on your career research. They might offer some advantages or disadvantages on specific careers that you haven't considered that you can add to your pros and cons list. If you need help starting a conversation with any of the adults in your life, see the section titled "Conversation."

Choose Up to Three Career Options

By the time you're finished listing the pros and cons of the careers you had on your original list, you should have a pretty good idea of your top career choice. If you still can't decide for sure, that's okay, but you do need to limit your options to no more than three. Otherwise, you won't be able to develop a feasible career plan that you can follow to reach your desired career. It's best to have one in mind when you get to this stage, but if you really can't choose, create a separate plan for up to three careers.

The next stage of planning involves setting goals and planning the education and training for your chosen career. If you have more than one career on your final list, you'll want to make a plan for each one because it's likely that they will all require a different educational path. If your careers are related, the education paths may also be similar. In a case like that, you can just note the differences that come up for each career while keeping your basic plan the same.

Set Goals

Before you move on to the education-planning stage, you'll start thinking about your lifetime goals. At your age, it might seem like you have all the time in the world to plan for things like retirement and lifetime achievements, but these years will go fast, and before you know it, you'll be applying for colleges, internships, or actual job roles. Setting goals now will help you keep your eye on the prize and guide you through your education and training to get you where you want to go.

Just because you set goals now doesn't mean you can't change them or choose a different path later. Your goals simply provide you with the framework for your intended career journey. Certainly, you'll need to make adjustments to your plan based on circumstances and unexpected events, but you shouldn't need to toss the whole thing out and start over, especially if you're determined to fulfill your career aspirations.

Even if you do decide to start over, you will have accomplished some steps along the way toward one career that you can apply to your new plan. Keeping them in mind will focus you and drive you to do everything you need to reach them.

College, Trade or Vocational School, or Specialty Programs

Based on your in-depth career research, your first goal will be to decide whether you want to attend college, enter a trade training program, or attend a specialty program. College encompasses junior colleges, which usually offer two-year associate's degrees, and full colleges and universities that offer bachelor's degrees, master's degrees, doctorates, and other advanced certifications.

Trade schools are often referred to as technical colleges or vocational schools. They specialize in training students for trade careers such as plumbing, information technology, electrical work, paralegal work, nursing, and more. You typically do not need to attend these schools for as long as a college or university program, but the careers they prepare you for also often require additional training after you earn your certificate. You may need to take a licensing or certification exam or serve time as an apprentice before you are considered fully trained.

A specialty program includes any post-secondary education that takes less than two years to complete. You won't receive a degree of any type from these programs, but you will receive the education and training you need to begin a career in that field. Programs like these include certificate programs in coding languages, media, technical areas (such as a pharmacy or cardiographic tech), court duties, security, and more. Some trades, like an HVAC technician, overlap the specialty program category, but the amount of education and on-the-job training you'll require as an applicant will vary by employer.

Most universities and colleges offer certificate programs that take less than two years to complete, but there are also specialty schools that focus on a single field. These are schools like the Colorado Media School, the New York Film Academy, the Culinary Institute of America, and the Connecticut Art School. Some of these certificate programs are more affordable than degree programs, and you are often able to start your career sooner as well. Be aware, though, that some companies require degrees for even entry-level positions, so before you choose a certificate program over a degree, be sure to verify the educational requirements for the job role you're pursuing.

Five-Year Vision

The next step in setting your career goals is to visualize your life five years after your high school graduation. While your post-secondary education might not take five or even four years to complete, the five-year benchmark is a good place to start with when setting a career goal. Take the time to answer these questions as you consider what your life will be like in five years:

- What type of job do I have?
- Is that job entry level or have I already moved up the career ladder?
- Do I still have additional education to complete to pursue my dream job?
- What does my daily routine look like in my job?
- What am I doing to advance in my job?
- Where do I live?
- What lifestyle do I have?
- If I went to a high school reunion, what would I tell people I do for a living?

The more specific and realistic you can be about your five-year vision, the better you can plan for it by setting up smaller goals on the way. Since career planning is all about creating a path toward your future career, you should have an end goal in mind. Of course, five years down the road from your high school graduation isn't the end of your career journey, but it's an important stop that allows you to check in on your progress.

Write down your answers to these questions so that you have a reference point throughout your career-planning process. If you don't write down your goals, it's easy for you to move the target or justify not reaching a smaller milestone. Writing down your goals also allows you to clarify them. Instead of just being dreams, your goals become more realistic when you see them on paper, and that will keep you motivated to reach them. ｜

10-Year Vision

Just as you did for five years after graduation, you'll now visualize what your life will be like 10 years after high school. Adding another five years to your career goals gives you time to advance from an entry-level position, gain more education for careers in medicine and law (which usually take significantly longer than a four-year degree), and settle into the life you ultimately want to live.

Again, write down the answers to these questions to clarify in your mind what you visualize yourself doing a decade after leaving high school.

- What type of job do I have?
- How many steps above entry level is this job?
- How many steps are left before I am in my dream job (or am I already there)?
- Do I still have additional education to complete to pursue my dream job?
- What does my daily routine look like in my job?
- What am I doing to advance in my job?
- What recognition have I received in my career field?
- Where do I live?
- What lifestyle do I have?
- If I went to a high school reunion, what would I tell people I do for a living?

Remember to keep your goals realistic and specific. You probably aren't going to be the top doctor in your field at 10 years after graduation, but you could be earning accolades that are trending toward that ultimate goal. It might be challenging for you to look ahead 10 years after high school, but it's an important step toward creating the career and life you want.

Ultimate Career Job Title and Position

Depending on your chosen career, you may want to set another milestone for 15 or 20 years after high school because you might need additional education and training years to reach your final goal. However, many people plan to achieve their ultimate career job title and position within 20 years after graduating. So, if you need additional milestone achievements, go ahead and add those to your plan, but be sure to define your ultimate career job title and position to keep it as your main focus.

The career job title and position you intend to achieve should be the pinnacle of your career planning. This is the title and position that you will be working toward from now until you achieve it, and once you achieve it, you will be living your dream. Of course, if you discover that there are even higher positions you want to gain as you work in your field for a few years, you can always add to your plan. For now, you want to set your sights on the position you intend to retire in. This doesn't mean you're locked into that position or can't add to your job duties, but it gives you something to aim for as you continue planning for your career.

Your ultimate job title and position might include a company that you hope to be working for, or it might be more general, especially if you eventually want to own your own company or work as a freelancer in your field. But, unless you have your heart set on working for a specific company — maybe you've always dreamed of being the editor of *Vogue* or you want to be the CEO of Coca Cola, for example — don't be too limiting on your ultimate title and position. You never know when an opportunity might arise that will lead to your dream career, and you don't want to turn it down because it's not the exact company you wanted.

Remember to consider things like the geography and lifestyle you prefer when you're choosing your ultimate job title and position. You may be able to reach a certain point in your career without those components, but they are important to your overall contentment with your life, so don't forget about them as you plan your career. Keep your priorities in mind so that your ultimate goal is in line with your values, interests, and other preferences.

Industry Awards and Accolades

Everyone wants to be recognized for their accomplishments, so along with thinking about your ultimate job title and position, you should also write down the industry awards and accolades you hope to achieve in this role. Certainly, winning these awards is not entirely within your control, but having them as goals along your journey will allow you to understand what you need to do to put yourself in the running.

Once you identify the industry awards you hope to achieve, write down the requirements for each award so that you can check them off as you accomplish them. Some awards, like lifetime achievement awards, can have vague requirements because they are awarded based on a person's entire body of work. You can't fully predict what your life's work will look like, but you can still choose an award like that as an ultimate goal and set the achievement of smaller awards that have more specific requirements along the way as milestone goals.

You also might not be able to predict certain industry accolades that you could get throughout your career, but you can make general goals. These might include having an article written about you or your work in an industry publication, being recognized at an industry event, or being nominated for a position in an industry advisory group. These are all accolades that indicate success in your position, and even more opportunities may arise throughout the years that you aren't expecting. You should still have an idea of the types of recognition you hope to eventually get, and work toward those goals.

Nearly all industries have their own major awards, even if they aren't as well-known as others, such as film awards. However, if your industry doesn't recognize excellence in a formal manner, you can still identify ways in which you can be a standout among your peers, even if it's just bringing more attention to what you do to the general public. Perhaps you can start a blog in your industry that clarifies what you do to help others, or maybe you can be a guest on podcasts to highlight your role in major projects. Whatever it is that brings you the recognition you want should be formalized as a goal during your planning process.

Retirement Age

At your age, you probably aren't thinking about retirement. After all, you're just getting started thinking about your career. However, retirement is a long-term goal that is wrapped up in the career-planning process. Most people don't want to work forever and intend to use the money they have saved throughout their career to live their life to the fullest during retirement. As such, it's vital that you have some idea of when you want to retire as you plan your career.

The official retirement age in the United States depends on when you can begin to collect Medicare benefits. With that said, there's no reason you can't retire earlier than the government considers normal if you have the funds to do so. And, if you don't want to retire at age 65, you don't have to, although there are some financial implications to this decision that we aren't going into here).

For most people, the earlier they can retire, the better; they want to live their lives without being tied to a job. But that's easier said than done. The majority of careers do not pay well enough to fund a significantly early retirement. Certainly, you can set a retirement age of 40 as your goal and work toward it, but setting a more realistic retirement age will allow you to get the most out of your career in terms of both satisfaction and money. For instance, if you have a 401(k) retirement fund with your employer, you will probably need at least 20 years (and probably closer to 30) in a job that supports 401(k)s to have built a retirement nest egg that can keep you in your desired lifestyle as a retiree.

Keep in mind that if you truly enjoy your career, you probably won't want to retire from it right away. This is part of the reason career planning is so important. You don't want to end up in a job that you hate and have to stick it out for years on end just to get to retirement. While this may be how other generations lived, you don't have to follow in their footsteps. For most careers, a reasonable retirement age is between 55 and 70 years old. You may still have to do some work if you retire at age 55 to ensure you have enough money to live on for the rest of your life, but with adequate planning, it's certainly feasible.

EDUCATION PLAN

Whenever you're designing a plan that encompasses numerous steps, start with the end in mind. This way, you can move backward to determine each step or mini-goal you need to accomplish to reach your end goal. By now, you've assessed your interests, values, talents, and other preferences. You've researched the careers you found interesting and that are aligned with your self-assessments. You've prioritized your options and narrowed your choices to between one and three careers. You've set your career milestones and written down your ultimate goals.

During your research, you found out what education is required to fulfill your career dreams. Now, you're ready to move backward a step and create an education plan to ensure you take all the classes and get all the certificates and degrees you need for a specific career. It's important to start your education plan as early as your freshman year in high school (9th grade) to guarantee you have all the prerequisite classes under your belt when it's time to enroll for the next set of classes. Otherwise, there could be a delay in achieving your goals.

Before we dive into the education-planning phase of your career plan, there are some terms you should be familiar with because they will be used regularly both in this guide and in your entire educational experience.

Core classes are those that all students are required to take before they graduate from high school. These are usually classes in the four major academic categories of English, math, social studies, and science. The core requirements vary by school district and sometimes by school, especially if you're in a private or charter school. In general, though, they're typically similar in that you need to take at least one English class per year for all four years, three or four math classes, three or four science classes, and two to four social studies classes. A physical education class and at least one year of a foreign language are also likely (although this is usually a college requirement and not a high school requirement).

Elective classes are those that students can choose to take and are typically geared toward specific interests. These classes always vary by school, with some standards like band, art, and physical education showing up on nearly every school's electives list. Other elective classes include wood and/or metal shop, automotive shop, culinary arts, computer science, keyboarding, coding, drama, photography, robotics, fashion design, jewelry, art, and many more.

Each class is worth a specific number of **credits**, and every student must satisfactorily complete a certain number to graduate. In the United States, this total number ranges from 13 to 24 credits. Keep in mind that not all states have four grades in their high schools, and not all follow the traditional two-semester school year, so 13 credits may be for a two- or three-year high school or a year-round high school. A class that is a semester long is usually worth 0.5 credits, so a full-year class would be worth 1 credit. In schools that use the traditional A–F grading scale, classes must be passed with at least a D to count toward a student's credit total.

Advanced Placement (AP) classes are courses you can take in high school that will potentially give you college credit or allow you to be placed in a more advanced class when you get to college.

For potential college credit, you are required to take an exam at the end of each course and achieve at least a three on a scale of one to five to earn that college credit or advanced placement. These classes may also be worth more credits than standard classes, which may depend on the score you achieve on the exam. For instance, an Advanced Placement biology class could be worth anywhere from one credit if you get a score of one or two on the exam to three credits for a score of four or five. It is important to remember that there is a cost to take the placement exam, and it is up to your future college whether they will accredit the AP exam or not.

Honors classes are those that move at a faster pace than standard classes and cover more material. They are usually reserved for students who demonstrate a specific talent in a subject and can also be AP classes. Not all honors classes are AP classes, so you may not get college credit. You can expect the workload of an honors class to be significantly higher than that of regular classes, with many more hours of homework per week. Many colleges and universities do look favorably upon students who have excelled in honors classes, especially schools that have a low acceptance rate and are highly competitive.

GPA stands for *grade point average*, a criteria that colleges, universities, trade schools, and specialty programs use to determine high school success. Traditionally, a grade of A is assigned four points, a B is assigned three points, a C is assigned two points, and a D is assigned one point. Your GPA is an average of all your grades throughout your high school career, with 4.0 being perfect. Some high schools offer more points for grades achieved in AP and honors classes, so it can be possible to get a GPA over 4.0 in some cases. It is important to note that not every high school follows this grading structure, so your scale could be different. The average college-bound student has a GPA of between 3.5 and 4.0, but there are many schools that accept a lower GPA.

Apprenticeships offer a career pathway that often bypasses formal education through degree and certificate programs. While you can have an apprenticeship at the same time that you're getting your post-secondary education, most companies are looking for people who want to earn while they learn. Many apprenticeships are offered to students interested in specific careers right out of high school, while others may require you to be enrolled in a degree or certificate program at the same time. The best part about an apprenticeship is that you get paid for the work you do while also learning the career.

Internships are different from apprenticeships in that they often do not provide a paycheck. You will gain valuable on-the-job experience and skills that will directly translate to your career. While you can find paid internships in some industries, they are rare, mostly because students are hungry for any opportunity to gain hands-on experience to make them more attractive candidates for career positions once they graduate from their post-secondary programs. Internships are often completed in the summer when students are not taking a full course load or after college graduation but before students obtain a full-time job.

Early High School (9th–10th Grades)

It's never too early to begin career planning, but normally, teens start the process somewhere around 9th or 10th grade during their freshman or sophomore years of high school. This is because, as you progress through your education, your class options become more specific to careers than the general classes you take in your first couple of years. Freshmen are usually required to take all the same core classes with one or two electives, but as you climb the grades, you are allowed to take fewer required classes and more electives.

Often, the electives are more career oriented, though not always. You'll still get a lot of value out of core classes for your career, especially if they're in the field you intend to pursue. For example, if you plan to become an English teacher, your core English classes will prove to be instrumental in the amount of background knowledge you need before you can teach the subject. The same is true for history, math, and science.

When you start high school, you will be assigned a counselor who will ensure you are taking the right number of credits to graduate on time. The first time you meet with your counselor one on one, let them know what your career plans are so that you can work together to schedule the classes that will put you in the best position to reach your career goals.

You won't have much choice in the classes you take as a freshman, but you can start planning for your sophomore year before enrollment starts late in the first semester or early in the second semester (for schools operating on the traditional two-semester school year). See the "Conversations" section for more information on questions to ask your counselor during these meetings.

Identify and Take High School Classes Related to Your Career

As previously mentioned, you will probably only have one elective per semester during your freshman year. Some lucky students might get two, but as more core classes are required, fewer electives are available in the early high school years. You probably enrolled in your electives while you were in 8th grade, so you likely just chose one or two that sounded interesting to you. That's perfectly fine, as it's not too important to take career-oriented classes as a freshman.

As soon as possible, though, take a look at your high school's course catalog (usually available online) to identify all the classes your school offers that are relevant to your desired career. A course catalog will list every class you can take in your school and provide a short description of what is covered in the class. It will also list the number of credits the class is worth and any classes you have to take and pass before you can enroll (prerequisites).

Make a list of the classes available that are relevant to your career, then group them based on when you can take them. For instance, you can take a 1-credit Drawing I class as a freshman, but you can't take a 1-credit Drawing II class until you complete Drawing I, so you can't take it until you're at least a sophomore. If you also want to take a 1-credit Drawing III and a 1-credit AP Art class, and each class requires the other before it is completed first, you'll have to list one each year to make sure you fit them all in.

You may not have a college, university, trade school, or specialty program in mind yet, but it doesn't hurt to also identify potential AP and honors classes that you can take in your years as an upperclassman to bolster your applications. If, eventually, you decide to attend a school that doesn't place an emphasis on AP and honors classes, you can always switch out these credits for other classes; for now, identifying them and temporarily placing them in your education plan will account for the most stringent university requirements.

There is also no need to take every single AP or honors class available. For one, you might not excel at all subjects, so taking an AP or honors course and not doing as well as you'd like could be worse than taking a regular class and getting a high grade. In fact, you probably won't be able to fit all of them in your schedule either. Focus on those that offer knowledge in your intended career area to demonstrate your commitment to learning everything you can about that field.

Identify and Join Clubs or Extracurricular Activities Related to Your Career

Not all learning happens in school, and not all schools will offer classes that are specifically geared toward your ultimate career goals. Plus, colleges and universities like to see extracurricular activities and club participation on your application because it shows you seek out additional opportunities to gain experience and knowledge. While these extracurricular activities and clubs don't necessarily have to be related to your career to impress college admissions personnel, they should be related to your career for your own personal gain.

Every club or activity you participate in that gives you more knowledge about your intended career will move you a step closer to your end goals. You'll also be able to get a better idea of the various positions and roles that are available to you in the field. These clubs and activities could end up changing your dream job title and career goal, but that's okay. Discovering this early on will allow you to fine tune your approach toward getting the education and experience you need to achieve your long-term objectives.

Many high schools offer noncredit clubs and extracurricular activities that are affiliated with the school and sponsored by school faculty but are held outside of school hours. Common clubs and extracurricular activities include less traditional athletic teams (ultimate Frisbee, golf, bowling, etc.), creative writing, e-sports, film, mock trial, Mathletics, Science Olympiad, yearbook, anime, model UN, political groups, fitness, D&D, religious groups, cheer, singing groups, book clubs, and hundreds more.

If you don't see a club that sparks your interest or is relevant to your career, your high school will usually have a process for starting a club. You will probably have to secure a faculty sponsor and a meeting place, but starting a club is not only a great way for you to gain valuable career experience but also an excellent way for you to showcase your leadership skills and initiative.

Another place to look for clubs that are not affiliated with your high school is websites for specific organizations and companies. For instance, if you're a female who is interested in engineering, you can visit the Society of Women Engineers website for resources on high-school-age clubs. Or you could check out the engineering club opportunities sponsored by Igus, a company that manufacturers high-performing plastics.

There are also a wide range of national clubs with local chapters that you can join, including Key Club, National Honor Society, DECA, National Art Honor Society, International Thespian Society, Science National Honor Society, Interact Club, and more. These clubs will usually have a formal process for starting a club in your area if there isn't one already, but most will already have a chapter you can join. There may be specific requirements to join these clubs, so be sure to research them before submitting an application.

Community colleges and community centers are other places that may have clubs and activities. These will usually require a fee but may have a wider selection available. Check out places like MeetUp.com and EventBrite to find other things to do outside of school. Just be sure to have an adult go with you at first to ensure your safety. These clubs may have older participants, especially if they are open to the entire community, so an adult should accompany you until it's determined that both the club and its location are safe.

Religious organizations will also have various clubs and activities you can participate in, so check with your place of worship for a list. You may need to join the organization or be a guest of a member before you can participate.

Finally, always check with your guardians before participating in a club or activity, even if it's affiliated with your school. Typically, these groups will require written permission from your guardians to ensure they are aware of your participation anyway, but even if they don't, getting your loved ones and friends involved can help enrich the experience.

Identify and Participate in Volunteer Opportunities Related to Your Career

In addition to clubs and extracurricular activities, you'll want to spend some of your time volunteering in areas that will provide you with more experience in aspects of your chosen career. Volunteering is another part of a well-rounded college application, and if it's related to your career, all the better.

Post-secondary schools and programs like to see that students can manage school, extracurricular activities, and volunteering while maintaining good grades. They also want to see that you're taking the initiative to help out your community in a way that's meaningful to you. Volunteering provides many chances to be a leader, which can make you stand out on your college applications, and if you're doing it as early as your freshman year, you can really demonstrate how you've made an impact on your community over time.

Many of the clubs that are available to you will include community service opportunities, including Key Club, National Honor Society, and others, but they may not be at all relevant to what you intend to do for a career. As such, you may need to identify volunteer opportunities on your own.

Fortunately, there is no shortage of volunteer opportunities in just about any field you can imagine. Want to become a veterinarian? Volunteer at your local animal shelter. Determined to be a construction manager? Volunteer with Habitat for Humanity. Looking to pursue a career in politics? Volunteer for a local candidate or campaign. Nearly all organizations that have a website that ends in .org have a page that outlines their volunteer opportunities and provides directions for how to become a volunteer.

Your place of worship will also have numerous opportunities for volunteering. While these opportunities usually have a religious component, they may still be aligned with your career aspirations. For example, if you're pursuing a career in medicine, volunteering with a church group that delivers medical services to underserved populations would be an excellent way to spend your time.

Be aware that in some instances, you may need to be a certain age before you can volunteer for some organizations. In other cases, you may be able to volunteer at a younger age if you're with an adult during your volunteer time. It really depends on the organization and their insurance requirements, so research is key before choosing a volunteer position.

Attend Summer Camps Related to Your Career

Summer camps present a terrific opportunity to experience aspects of your desired career or industry over an extended period of time. Usually, summer camps last between one week and two months, and they can be day camps or overnight. While camps can be expensive, you might be able to get a scholarship to attend if you're unable to afford the full tuition.

Traditionally, summer camps are about water activities, crafts, athletics, and other non-career pursuits, but if you're intentional about the summer camp you select, you can find one that will help you gain experience in your preferred area. CollegeMajor.com has an excellent list of career-exploration summer camps that range from a National History camp to an American Psychology Association camp and everything in between.

TeenLife.com also maintains a list of career-exploration summer camp opportunities, many of which are also listed on the CollegeMajor list, but there are some variations between the two. These are national camps, so be sure to apply early and get your tuition in. There are likely local summer camps in your area that are geared toward careers, so ask your high school counselor to help you research the options. Local camps will usually be less expensive for in-state attendees, especially if you don't have to pay for travel to get there.

Other sources of career-related summer camps are college websites. Many universities and colleges host high school summer camps to introduce their campus to potential applicants. You'll be able to find camps that take advantage of the resources these colleges have at their fingertips, which can mean you get hands-on experience in your career that you wouldn't get otherwise. Check the websites of in-state colleges and universities first, then expand your search to out-of-state colleges to get an idea of the types of camps available to you.

Museums, zoos, and other attractions often host camps that allow you to attend programs throughout the day but come home at night. These are usually more affordable than overnight camps because you don't pay for lodging or food, although lunch is sometimes included in the cost. Day camps are also more limited in what you learn. Still, they offer valuable career-related experiences that you can't get in school.

If you aren't able to attend an entire camp, you may have the opportunity to attend a shorter session. Most camps offer various intervals to accommodate more students. Remember that summer camps fill up fast because parents want to ensure their kids have something to do during their time off from school. Begin your research early, and apply as soon as possible to several camps that offer career-related content to have the best chances of getting into one you want.

It must be said here that you should take care not to overload yourself with activities, clubs, volunteering, and camps because you simply can't do everything and do it well. Be intentional about the activities and clubs you choose so that you aren't overwhelmed with scheduling nightmares. In fact, if you can only participate in one, that's perfectly okay, especially right now as you're establishing yourself in high school and determining your career path.

As far as volunteering goes, you don't have to select a recurring opportunity. You can simply choose a day and volunteer a single time. Your efforts will be much appreciated, and after you're done, you can decide whether you want to make it a more permanent activity or not. You can even try several volunteer opportunities for different causes or organizations to get a wide range of experiences in your field (and out of your field, if you wish). If you're passionate about a cause or an organization, you can also volunteer in several roles to experience different aspects of a career or industry.

Overscheduling can lead to burnout, so don't jump into every single opportunity that comes your way. This is why you should make a list of possibilities before choosing the clubs, activities, volunteer opportunities, and camps that make the most sense for your career and education plan.

Mid–High School (10th and 11th Grades)

Once you start 10th grade (sophomore year), you should be well into your career and education plan. If you think about it, you only have three years until you're expected to either go to college or trade school or begin working. It might seem like a long way off, but it's really not. Consider how fast your middle school years went. That's how quickly your high school experience is going to go as well.

Your years in 10th and 11th grade will be packed with career-exploration opportunities, but if you've already decided on a career path, you are ahead of the game. You may still want to participate in organized career events, especially if they're offered through your high school, but your focus should be on furthering your education plan to put you in the best possible position to enter your field of choice when it's time.

Continue Taking High School Classes Related to Your Career

We won't completely rehash the importance of taking high school classes related to your career in this section since we already expounded on this topic earlier. But it's important enough that it needs to be reiterated so that you keep your eye on the prize: You should have a basic outline of classes you need to take and want to take throughout high school to ensure you get everything in before you graduate. Follow that outline as long as you are progressing toward your goals.

In some cases, a high school will start offering new classes at the beginning of each academic year. Evaluate each new offering and decide if it fits into your overall education plan. If it does, shuffle your class outline around to accommodate the new course. You may have to make some difficult decisions during this process as you decide which classes will be more beneficial to you in the future.

Other classes may be terminated before you get an opportunity to take them, so make sure you review your school's course catalog before every enrollment period. Elective classes are usually offered based on interest and enrollment; if a class isn't filling up, it could be cut from the catalog. If this happens, reassess the offerings at your school and make an alternative choice. It might not be directly related to your career, but even if it's tangentially related, it will be of value to you.

Continue Participating in Clubs or Extracurricular Activities Related to Your Career

Again, this is not a topic we need to go into depth about at this stage because we already did so earlier. You'll want to continue participating in clubs or extracurricular activities that are propelling you toward your career. By this time, you may have taken on a leadership role with your club or activity, which is another wonderful way to stand out on future applications.

Continue looking for new opportunities to get involved in clubs or activities that are related to your career, even if you don't actively participate in them. They are options for you if you decide to take on more responsibilities, and you could find better matches since new opportunities arise all the time. Just be sure you wrap up your outstanding duties with an existing club or activity before you choose a new one.

Continue Participating in Volunteer Opportunities Related to Your Career

It's not enough to volunteer just once in your high school career if you want to impress post-secondary educational institutions or gain meaningful experience that you can apply to your career. You need to continually search out and participate in volunteer opportunities throughout your high school years. While you don't have to make one specific volunteer opportunity a regular gig, you do need to make volunteering in general a habit.

As was mentioned previously, you may want to try a variety of volunteer roles in a single organization or volunteer with multiple organizations and causes relevant to your career field. A good rule of thumb is to volunteer once a month with an organization or cause for a few hours on the weekend or after school.

Some high schools require a minimum number of volunteer hours for graduation, and most service-oriented clubs mandate a set number of volunteer hours to maintain membership. Documenting your volunteer hours is good practice to ensure you meet these requirements and to demonstrate your commitment to volunteerism on your future applications.

Identify and Apply to Part-Time Jobs Related to Your Career

Once you reach approximately 15 years old, you can start to work at various companies in your community. Mostly, the jobs you will be eligible for are entry-level positions at fast food restaurants, retail stores, and entertainment venues. But there may be entry-level part-time positions available at companies in your desired field. The main barrier to getting a part-time job in your career area is that working hours are often the same as school hours. However, it definitely doesn't hurt to start looking for these positions by searching online job boards like Indeed, Monster, Craigslist, and others.

The point of a part-time job in high school, other than earning your own money, which is a good enough reason on its own, is to start gaining experience that will serve you well in any field you choose once you graduate. If you work in fast food or retail, you'll learn how to deal with customers, use a cash register, count change, and maintain cleanliness. You'll also be exposed to marketing strategies, organizational methods, approaches to time management, and hierarchical responsibilities. These soft skills are critical to any career, and all high school students should learn the basics of these skills by the time they graduate.

If possible, try to land a part-time job that will give you additional experience in your career of choice, even if it's not the main focus. For example, if you are interested in a marketing career, working at a retail store will give you valuable insights into how a company markets its products to potential customers. While you'll have to perform your assigned job duties, you can also ask questions about the career-related aspects of your job. Even fast food companies need to advertise, so learning about those strategies will provide additional career-related knowledge that you can add to your ever-growing arsenal.

You might not be able to find a part-time job that is in any way connected to your career of choice, especially if you want a career in a field that requires you to be in a different location than where you currently live. In that case, choose a part-time job that you find interesting so that you remain engaged with your responsibilities throughout your time there. Try to stay at a single job for a year or longer to demonstrate your ability to commit to a position, follow the company's rules, and perform the necessary job functions at a competent level.

All part-time jobs are critical for your future resume, so take careful note of the job functions you perform and the skills you're using on a daily basis. Even if they're not directly relevant to your desired career, the soft skills you learn on any job will translate to just about any career. Employers want to know that you're trainable, can learn new systems and skills quickly, and can persevere during challenges that always arise in any position.

Identify Post-Secondary Institutions with Degrees or Certificates in Your Career

You should begin looking at colleges, universities, trade schools, and specialty programs that offer degrees or certificates in your career no later than the end of your sophomore year. This is because you'll often need to take certain courses in your junior and senior years of high school to be eligible for post-secondary programs. If you don't take these classes while in high school, you'll have to take them at a community college before you can be admitted to the post-secondary school of your choice. Although this is not always the case, it is important to see it is a good idea to research your dream schools' requirements early on.

Start by researching the post-secondary educational opportunities in your own state, especially if your career lends itself to the geography or climate you already live in. Educational institutions will often offer special tuition rates for local residents, so if cost is a major concern and you don't think you'll get a full scholarship, you will do yourself a great favor by attending school at an in-state program. Alternatively, you can start your post-secondary education at an in-state school and transfer to a program more appropriate for your career at an out-of-state school for your years as an upperclassman.

Next, expand your research to out-of-state schools and programs that offer specific career tracts. It can be challenging to find an exact career tract at an in-state school, especially if you choose a more obscure career. For instance, if you want a degree in an e-sports field, there are fewer than 15 colleges and universities that offer this specific career tract. If that's the case, you will need to attend one of the schools that offers your preferred program or find an alternate path to your goal. As previously mentioned, you can always start your education at an in-state school and transfer to one that has the program you desire.

All things considered, it's usually better to start and end your post-secondary education with the same institution, at least for your first certificate or degree. This is because you don't have to worry about whether or not your credits at one institution will transfer to another or if you'll need to take additional core classes at the second institution before you'll be able to graduate.

So, if you have the funds available and are academically eligible for a specific career program at an out-of-state school, it's advisable to enroll in that program with a start date for the first term after high school ends (usually the fall term). Additionally, by researching post-secondary educational programs this far in advance of actually applying, you can set up mini-goals toward the major goal of being accepted by and being able to afford your program of choice, even if it's out of state.

For more adventurous students, you may even want to consider international post-secondary programs. These will typically be more expensive than either in-state or out-of-state schools, but they may also have programs you can't access in the United States. For example, if you plan to pursue a career in a foreign language, attending post-secondary school in a country that speaks that language is an extremely valuable experience. Plus, it will be a bonus skill you can add to your ever-growing resume when you apply for jobs in your career field. Global studies, international affairs, political science, international education, and international relations are other popular career paths that students study in international schools.

Be aware that international post-secondary educational degree programs often don't offer the flexibility of changing your major once you enroll. You need to have a specific career path that you're committed to following before you commit. If you are at all unsure about your career path, stay in the U.S. until you've firmly made a decision. This way, you aren't wasting your money on a program you have no intention of using once you graduate.

If you can, visit the college or university campuses that are on your shortlist. In-state campuses shouldn't be too difficult to visit, and doing so will give you a better idea of what it would be like to attend that school. Out-of-state and international schools are more challenging to visit, but if you're able to actually set foot on campus, it could really help you make your decision.

Schools usually have scheduled tours for prospective students that are listed on their website. If possible, try to line up your campus visit with one of these scheduled tours. While you can certainly visit a campus on your own, you will really benefit from an insider's tour of the facilities. You'll learn more about the campus itself and discover where things are that you might not find from exploring the campus yourself.

There are also virtual campus visits that will give you a tour of the facilities at schools you can't visit in person. Check the school's website for live-visit dates, or take the time to watch a recorded visit. While a virtual tour is better than no tour at all, it's still preferable to check out a campus in person if you can to get a better idea of the culture and community.

A note about apprenticeships: If you're planning to go directly from high school into an apprenticeship, you need to make those arrangements well ahead of your graduation. In fact, it's a good idea to start looking for a company that will offer an apprenticeship in your career of choice as soon as possible. The best place to start your research is at the Apprenticeship.gov Career Seeker's page, which offers information about apprenticeships and features an apprenticeship job-finder tool.

Apprenticeships may or may not require additional post-secondary education, but each opportunity is different. Be sure to read the requirements of any apprenticeship opportunity you find on this or any other website. Some apprenticeships can also be completed while you're getting your post-secondary education, so it never hurts to check out these jobs even if you're also pursuing a degree or certificate.

Determine the Educational Requirements for Post-Secondary Programs

Once you identify the post-secondary programs you're interested in pursuing, you need to outline the educational requirements that will allow you to apply and get accepted into your desired programs. Not every college, university, trade school, or specialty program has the same requirements, and unless you choose a junior or community college, trade school, or specialty program, you'll need more than just a high school diploma.

Pay attention to the following requirements for each program you're considering:

- GPA: This will need to be maintained from your freshman year until you graduate
- Required high school classes: While these should be more or less the same classes as what you are required to take to graduate from high school, some universities or colleges

look more favorably upon students who take AP and honors courses in addition to or in place of regular classes. Additionally, most colleges require at least a semester of a foreign language class, even though this is not usually a high school graduation requirement.

- Required entrance exams: Most four-year colleges and universities require adequate scores on one of the two major standardized tests, the Scholastic Aptitude Test (SAT) or the American College Test (ACT). While there are now more than 1,000 post-secondary four-year degree programs that no longer require these tests, they are still the gold standard for most schools. Junior colleges, community colleges, trade schools, and specialty programs usually do not require scores from these or any other tests because they are open-admission schools. Four-year colleges and universities that do not require entrance exam scores usually do require a portfolio from your high school classes that demonstrates your readiness for college.

Note Application Deadlines

While you won't be applying to these post-secondary programs until the summer before or the fall of your senior year of high school, you should be familiar with their application deadlines. These deadlines will change each year, but they should be consistently around the same time so that you can start planning your application process.

Some educational institutions offer an early-admission deadline that allows students to apply much earlier and get a decision faster than the standard admissions process. The advantage of this is that both you and the school can count on your acceptance, which is usually binding, meaning you can't accept any other offer from another school later.

In fact, if you accept an early decision offer, you are required to withdraw all applications from other schools. This option should only be for those students who absolutely have a first choice for where they want to go to college and have no doubt about attending the program in the fall. The big drawback to early admission is that you may not know if there will be financial assistance available when you're required to make your decision, and you won't be able to accept financial aid, including scholarships, from other schools once you've committed to a program through early decision.

That being said, there is no *legally* binding contract that prevents you from backing out of an early-admission commitment. The school is unlikely to pursue you for lost tuition, especially if the reason you don't commit is related to financial aid. However, your decision can affect your high school's reputation, so it shouldn't be a decision you take lightly.

Keep in mind that a university or college program has a predetermined number of available enrollment slots each year. The earlier you apply, the better your odds are for getting one of these openings, especially if you're a standout candidate. If you have your heart set on attending a specific program that will lead to your dream career, circle that application deadline on your calendar to ensure you keep yourself focused on achieving that goal.

Note Application Fees

Most post-secondary education degree programs have an application fee that falls between $50 and $90 and is used to offset admission costs like reading through applications and sending out acceptance and denial letters. These fees are assessed to ensure that only students who are serious about attending their programs apply. For this reason, you will find that highly selective schools charge higher application fees than schools that are competing for fewer students or have many enrollment slots available.

Community colleges, junior colleges, trade schools, and specialty programs are less likely to have application fees, but some still do require them as a means of covering admission costs. Since many of these schools are open admissions and will accept any student with a high school diploma or equivalent, they don't charge you to apply to their programs. But, when a class is full, you'll have to go on the waitlist and hope someone drops out before classes start.

By noting the application fees ahead of time, you can save up to pay for them when it's time to actually apply. Keep in mind that when you apply to five or six schools, you could pay up to $500 in application fees alone. These are nonrefundable fees, so even if you don't get accepted into a program, you won't get that money back. However, you can request a waiver of these fees based on your financial situation. If you're in a position where you can't afford the application fees, research the school's fee-waiver request process to be considered.

Note Tuition and Room and Board Costs

Just because you're accepted at a specific school doesn't mean you can afford to attend. Unfortunately, post-secondary education is expensive, and it's getting even more expensive every year. You will need to think about how you're going to pay for your education beyond high school, and it's never too early to begin. Most students will have to use a combination of student loans and scholarships to pay for their degrees or certificates, but there may be other options available to you depending on your financial situation.

This is definitely a conversation you need to have with your parents since they will likely play a large role in how you pay for post-secondary education. They may need to help you take out a loan or secure specific income-based grants. They may even have saved for your college tuition since you were a baby, which would be a wonderful surprise!

If you're a sophomore or junior in high school, you don't have to worry about paying for tuition and room and board just yet, but you should get an idea of how much a full course load at each school you're considering will cost in the event you're accepted and decide to attend.

Currently, the average cost of a single college credit at a public in-state four-year university or college in the U.S. is $390. Since most college classes are three credits, this means you'll pay an average of $1,170 for a semester-long college course. Private in-state four-year colleges and universities have an average credit hour cost of $1,365, or $4,095 per class. Out-of-state colleges and universities run $1,126 per credit, or $3,378 per class. Community college courses are significantly less expensive, coming in at an average of $141 per credit hour, or $423 per course.

These fees do not include room (lodging), board (food), books, or supplies. Room and board for public institutions, whether in state or out of state, averages $487 per credit hour, so if you're taking 12 credit hours to be considered a full-time college student, you will pay an average of $5,844 per semester for lodging and food. Books and supplies average $51 per credit hour for public and private four-year institutions.

In total, with tuition, room, board, books, and other expenses, full-time students pay an average of $1,099 per credit hour at public in-state institutions and $1,835 per credit hour at out-of-state institutions. This ultimately reaches a total of $13,188 per semester for an in-state education and $22,020 per semester for an out-of-state education. At a private institution, the cost goes up to an average of $2,194 per credit hour, or $26,328 per semester.

Conversely, a two-year public community college that doesn't offer room and board charges an average of $344 per credit hour. You'll want to be careful to check if this price includes books and supplies while planning and budgeting. This equates to a total of $4,128 per semester for a full 12-hour course load. With the savings you can get by choosing a two-year program over a four-year program, you may want to consider attending a two-year school for your core classes and transferring to a four-year school for your career-specific classes and your degree.

Remember that these are only averages. Some schools will be significantly less expensive, while the more prestigious schools are going to be well over the average costs. Once you determine how much the schools you're considering charge, you will want to have additional conversations with your parents and high school guidance counselor to find ways to help you attend the school of your choice.

You also do not have to take a full course load unless your financial aid requires it. If you're paying out of pocket for your fees, you can take fewer credits at a time to make it more affordable. Of course, this means it will take you longer to graduate, but if it's the only way you can pay for your education, it's better than accepting a career you don't really want because you aren't able to satisfy the educational requirements of your dream career.

Identify Scholarship Opportunities, Requirements, and Deadlines

One way to pay for at least part of your tuition and other expenses for a post-secondary program is to be awarded scholarships that cover a certain dollar amount. There are all types of scholarships available, so you should be able to identify some that you are eligible to apply for based on your interests, talents, demographics, academic level, career path, and more.

Some scholarships may not require an application, but most do, so you need to be aware of those that are available to avoid accidentally missing the deadline. There are numerous websites that offer scholarship searches for free. You shouldn't have to pay for anyone to find them for you.

In fact, the U.S. Department of Labor operates a free scholarship search tool that has a database of nearly 9,000 scholarships and their criteria that you can access any time. Use various filters like location, keywords, education level, and scholarship type to refine your search and obtain more relevant results. Smaller, local scholarships may not be listed on this website, so be sure to also inquire about any scholarships your guidance counselor is aware of to help you compile your own list of scholarships you're going to apply for.

As you list your scholarship opportunities, be sure to note the requirements and deadlines so that you don't waste your time applying for scholarships you're not eligible for. Keep in mind that while most scholarships are offered every year, some aren't. As such, it's important to keep checking various scholarship databases to identify new opportunities and cross off ones that are no longer available.

Most scholarships will not require an application fee, but some might. You'll need to weigh the scholarship opportunity against the fee they charge to determine whether or not it's worth it to apply. An application fee serves as a way to ensure only the most serious applicants apply. If you're not willing to pay the fee, it's probably not a good match for you; after all, there are plenty of scholarships that don't charge an application fee.

Scholarship applications often require an essay, and those that don't usually have many more applicants than those that do, making them more difficult to get. When you're researching scholarship opportunities, make note of which ones require an essay and this year's topic to get an idea of what you'll have to write about when it comes time for you to apply. You can also practice writing scholarship application essays by using this year's topics. Have your guidance counselor or English teacher look over your practice essays to help strengthen your writing skills before you apply.

Late High School (11th and 12th Grades)

When you reach the midpoint of your junior year (11th grade) in high school, it's time to get serious about your career path, if you haven't already. Keep in mind that it's recommended you really start planning your career when you're in 9th or 10th grade, if not before. That doesn't mean you have to know exactly what you want to do, but you should be narrowing down your options. By the second semester of 11th grade, you should have a solid plan in place for what you're going to do when you graduate from high school.

Continue Taking High School Classes Related to Your Career

As with your sophomore and junior years, you will continue taking high school classes related to your career. By the time you're in 11th grade, you may be finished with most of your required core classes, opening up time for you to take additional electives. This is an excellent opportunity for you to add experience and knowledge to your career toolkit. Again, the more you learn now, the better prepared you'll be in your post-secondary education and early career.

You might be tempted to have additional "off periods" where these core classes once used to be. Certainly, you deserve some time during your day for things you want to do rather than things you have to do, but if you're determined to be in the best position possible for your career, taking additional career-oriented electives instead of having an off period is recommended. You'll probably never get another opportunity to take classes for free at a time when you also don't have a full-time job to worry about.

In addition to taking electives, be sure you are also fulfilling the course requirements you need to be eligible to attend the college or university of your choice. If you miss one, you'll have to take it on your own before you can enroll in your post-secondary program, which means you'll probably have to pay for it out of your own pocket. Unless you can get the class in during the summer before college starts in the fall, you'll end up delaying the start of your career.

Continue Participating in Clubs or Extracurricular Activities Related to Your Career

As you get closer to graduation, your time will fill up quickly, and you might discover you need to drop a club or two. This is perfectly fine, but you would be wise not to drop all of them. Colleges and employers look at clubs and extracurricular activities on applications to determine candidates who went out of their way to gain career experience even when they didn't have to. They also want to see you take on leadership roles in these clubs and activities, and by your senior year, if you've been in the club for a few years, you will probably be in a position to become a leader.

Now may not be the time to take on additional clubs or activities, although if you find one that is a perfect fit for your career aspirations, by all means join it. You just don't want to spread yourself too thin as you prepare for the next phase in your career planning because there will be a lot to do to get to the next level.

Continue Participating in Volunteer Opportunities Related to Your Career

As you are able, continue volunteering with organizations or causes that are giving you career experience. Your time will be limited in your junior and senior years, but colleges and universities like to see that you continued to set aside time to help others throughout your entire high school experience. They want to know that giving back is a priority for you even if you're also getting personal value in return.

In other words, you may have to cut back on the time you spend volunteering when things get busy, but don't give it up altogether. It's an important aspect of a well-rounded post-secondary application, and you need to demonstrate that you find volunteer experience valuable even when your life gets hectic.

Continue Working Part-Time Jobs to Build Your Resume

If you haven't already obtained a part-time job, this is the time to do it. Not only will you be earning your own money, but you'll also be gaining valuable skills in a low-risk environment. Companies that hire high school students know they will need to spend time training those employees in even the most basic of skills. This is your chance to acquire skills you will need for any position you hold in the future.

If you can find a part-time job that is related to your preferred career, that is the best-case scenario, but don't limit yourself to such a job. Your main goal is to start building your resume so that future employers can see that you are able to hold a job, can learn new systems and skills quickly, and are able to work within a defined structure (i.e., you can follow their rules). Try not to jump around from job to job too much either. Employers are looking for long-term employees, and they aren't going to hire and train someone just for that person to leave right away.

Almost all jobs have common soft skills that will be required for a lifetime. You're not wasting your time at a high school job, even if it's not directly related to your career goals. You are learning how to work for someone else, although you might learn that you don't want to work for someone else, and you're learning how to interact with customers. You're also learning practical skills like getting to work on time, taking initiative, working as part of a team, completing tasks, meeting deadlines, and other skills that will serve you well no matter what career you end up in.

Take All Required Entrance Exams

Most students will take the SAT exam for the first time in the spring of their junior year. If you don't get a score you're happy with, you can take it again on your own time, but most U.S. high schools require juniors to sit for this test as part of their high school curriculum. If you know you're not going to go to a four-year college or university that requires the SAT, your parents can opt you out of taking the exam in high school, but it's always a good idea to know your score for your own personal knowledge.

Some post-secondary schools also accept scores from the ACT exam, but high schools don't always offer a formal opportunity to take this exam as part of a curriculum. You will probably need to register for it and take it on your own, but it can offer a better picture of all your knowledge because, unlike the SAT, the ACT assesses students in English, writing, reading, math, and science instead of just English and math. Not all schools accept this test, though, so make sure you know which scores have to be submitted to which schools.

There are fees to take both the SAT and ACT exams. The SAT is $55 as long as you register on time. If you are a late registrant, the cost is $85. The ACT is $63 without the writing portion and $88 with the writing portion. You may be able to get these fees waived based on your financial situation. The instructions for requesting a fee waiver are on each exam's website.

The testing companies will automatically send your scores to colleges and universities of your choice, if you wish. For instance, both the SAT and ACT allow up to four free score reports per registered exam, and you can choose where to send these reports for up to nine days after you take the test. Additional score reports are $12 each for the SAT and $16 each for the ACT. If you take these exams in the spring of your junior year and are satisfied with your scores, you may need to request additional score reports once you determine which schools you're applying to.

Apply to Post-Secondary Educational Programs

The big step is here! In the summer before or during the fall of your senior year, you should begin applying to the post-secondary educational programs you identified during your sophomore and junior years. The application deadlines will have changed some, so be sure to double check the new deadline dates and note them prominently to avoid forgetting them. Early decision deadlines are typically in November, so if you want to apply for early admission, you'll definitely need to start the process in the summer before your senior year.

Regular admission deadlines vary but can be as early as November 30 and as late as March 15. However, most schools have an application deadline of January 1 of the new year. Just be sure you're very clear on when the absolute last day is that you can submit your application for your desired school because they are not flexible on this date at all. If you miss it, you will have to wait until next year to apply.

Some schools do have what is known as rolling admissions, which means they accept applications at all times and evaluate them as they are received. They will continue to accept applications until all student slots are filled for the year. Generally, junior colleges, community colleges, trade schools, and specialty programs follow a rolling-admissions model. Some of these schools also have multiple term start dates so that if you miss one start date, you'll be able to catch the next one.

Applying to colleges and universities is easier than it's ever been thanks to the internet. The Common App is a popular way to apply to multiple colleges without filling out multiple applications. The Common App is accepted by more than 900 schools, but keep in mind that most colleges and universities have a supplemental section of the Common App that includes school-specific requirements. You will still need to pay a separate application fee for each school you send the Common App to, but at least you won't have to fill out your basic information more than once.

Schools that don't accept the Common App will post their application requirements on their website. You should have already researched their requirements earlier in your planning process, but if you haven't, be sure to carefully follow all the requirements when you apply so that your application isn't rejected.

The most daunting part of a college application is the essay or "personal statement." There will be a different prompt for each institution, but your response will need to be around 650 words in length and directly related to the prompt. You will usually have more than one prompt to choose from, so be sure to select the one that will best demonstrate your communication and writing skills. Your essay should also be self-reflective and show insight into yourself and your experiences.

Fortunately, you can have another person look over your essays and personal statements before you submit your applications. Take advantage of this! Have your English teacher or guidance counselor help you work out your ideas and offer advice on content and mechanics. Be careful to keep the essay in your voice and make sure it clearly expresses your ideas so that you're assessed on your own skills and no one else's.

Most four-year colleges and universities also require you to submit letters of recommendation with your applications. Typically, you will need to get at least two and sometimes three letters of recommendation from teachers and counselors. These letters should be requested at least two months in advance of when you intend to apply. This gives the people you're requesting the letters from plenty of time to compose a thoughtful and complimentary letter.

You'll want these letters to come from the teachers and counselors who know you best and can comment on your work ethic and academic aptitude. If you are applying for a program that is specific to your career aspirations, you'll want a letter of recommendation from a teacher who can attest to your desire and aptitude for that career. If you are working part-time in a career-related job, you should also request a letter of recommendation from a supervisor who can talk about your passion and aptitude for the field.

Letters of recommendation should never come from your family or friends. After all, they are biased and would probably say whatever they need to say to ensure you get into the college or university of your choice. They would only be trying to help, but admissions officials would disregard these letters. Choose letters from teachers, counselors, and supervisors instead to lend credibility to your applications.

Choose a Post-Secondary Program After Receiving Acceptance Letters

Now comes the waiting game. After you've applied to the post-secondary programs you want to attend, you have little to do but wait for their replies. This can be challenging, especially if your heart is set on going to a specific college or university. If you applied for early admission, you should receive a decision letter in December, January, or February. If you applied for regular admission, you can expect to get your decision letters by mid-March or April. Of course, the later the deadline, the later the decision, so keep that in mind as well.

College decision letters aren't always actual letters either, although most colleges and universities will follow up an email or portal notification with an official letter delivered to your home address. The colleges and universities you applied to will let you know how they will deliver their decision so that you can keep an eye on the right place.

If you've applied to multiple schools, you will need to keep track of when the decisions are expected and the date by which you have to accept an offer. A good way to do this is to list all the schools you applied to on a spreadsheet along with their decision and acceptance deadlines. You can also compare other aspects of each school on this spreadsheet as well, like tuition costs, especially if you're still undecided about where you want to go.

When you've received all the decisions from the colleges and universities you've applied to, it's time to make your choice. You won't have too long to decide because most schools will require a decision within about a month of their acceptance. By now, you should have a first choice, and if you've been accepted to that school, go ahead and fill out the required acceptance form and send in your deposit (usually between $50 and $500) to secure your spot.

Apply for Scholarships and Grants

Once you've accepted an offer from a post-secondary school, you might think you can relax. Well, you don't have to worry about which school you're going to attend anymore, but unless you can pay the tuition, room, and board fees out of pocket, you'll still have more work to do. You'll need to research financial aid options through the school you're attending and, if necessary, apply for loans that will cover these expenses.

At the same time, you should be applying for any scholarships and grants you qualify for to help minimize your expenses. In most cases, you'll be able to apply for and accept as many scholarships as possible to lower your overall costs. Be sure to pay attention to all application deadlines and requirements so that your application isn't tossed out due to a technicality.

Additionally, when you're offered a scholarship, you need to accept it by the stated deadline in your offer letter. If you do not accept the scholarship by that deadline, the money will go to someone else. Keep in mind that some scholarships have contingencies attached to them. For instance, some might only be offered if you pursue a specific career. Others might only be good if you go to a specific school. If you're offered scholarships that have these contingencies, make sure you will be able to fulfill their requirements before you accept the money.

Keep checking for new scholarships and grants that come up even after you've decided where you're going to school. Until or unless you get your entire tuition, room, and board covered, every little bit of money you can get to pay down your debt will be welcome. It takes a lot of effort to keep applying for scholarships and grants, but it's entirely worth it.

Post-High School: Trade School, Specialty Programs, and Apprenticeships

You've graduated high school and you're ready to take on the world. You're not attending a four-year college or university but instead have elected to attend a trade school or specialty program or participate in an apprenticeship. This is a perfectly acceptable route to a career, and you should be commended for knowing what you want to do and setting out to do it.

Trade schools and specialty programs often have multiple start dates throughout the year. As such, you can usually choose when you want to start your post-secondary education. It's advisable to take the summer off between your senior year and starting your post-secondary education because you will never get that opportunity again, and most of your peers will be on a similar schedule.

Attending a trade school or specialty program offers significant benefits to students. For one, you will be guided through the process as you learn about your career so that you'll know when it's time to take your licensing and certification exams. All steps that need to be taken for you to start your career as soon as you finish the program will be included in your education. Your school will also have a job assistance center or program that can help you find a job in your career after you're finished with the program in most cases.

Instead of attending a trade school or specialty program, you might be ready to jump into an apprenticeship to gain on-the-job experience while earning a paycheck. In many instances, even if you do go to a trade school, you'll need to have an apprenticeship as well before you can be certified and licensed. If you're at a school, your counselor will be able to help you find an apprenticeship.

If you're not attending a trade school or specialty program, you will need to apply for an apprenticeship through a site like Apprenticeship.gov or a state-specific apprenticeship site. Alternatively, you can check with local businesses in your field of choice to enter into an apprenticeship with one of them. In most cases, you will have to take some classes at the same time as your apprenticeship before you can get your license or certification. If you commit to working for the company after your apprenticeship is over, they may pay for these classes.

Licensing and certification exams are usually offered through industry-specific organizations or formal testing companies. They will require a fee, and some have restrictions on how often you can take the exams if you don't pass the first time. You may also have to accrue continuing education credits to keep your license and certification valid, so be sure to check all requirements and follow them throughout your career.

Early Post-Secondary

As a freshman in college, you will likely be overwhelmed at everything you have to do to just stay afloat at school. You'll probably be taking mostly core classes that are required for everyone to graduate, regardless of career or field. This is just like it was when you were a freshman in high school. There may be specific requirements that you must complete in English, math, science, social studies, and physical education before you can receive your degree. You will take most of these core classes in your freshman and sophomore years.

You will also need to designate a major, which should be directly tied to your career choice. This will set you on a path that ensures you take every class necessary to satisfy the minimum requirements for a degree in that field. You will be assigned a counselor or advisor who will guide you through your course selection as you progress in college. They will ensure you are on pace for graduation, whether that's in the traditional four years or on the five-year plan.

Declaring your major early in your college experience will allow you to graduate on time. If you change majors at any point, you will probably have to take additional courses to fulfill the new major's requirements. This causes a delay in your education, but if the plan you've created isn't working for you, a change in your major might be necessary.

Be aware that your undergraduate major may not be the same as your career. For example, if you intend to be an FBI agent, you won't major in joining the FBI. Instead, you'll focus on criminal justice, computer science, forensics, psychology, or law, depending on what you want to do as an FBI agent. You also may need an advanced degree to meet your career goals. For instance, doctors often get an undergraduate degree in pre-med, biology, or anatomy before getting their advanced degree in medicine or more specific medical fields such as cardiology, pathology, or pediatrics, etc.

Take Required Classes to Progress Toward Degree or Certification

As an underclassman, your focus will be on taking your required classes, both core and major-specific. While many of these may not seem relevant to your desired career, they are necessary to provide the educational foundation for many of the more specific classes you take later on. Just as your high school grade point average began as a freshman, your college GPA begins as a freshman in college. These classes do count toward your GPA and degree, so take them seriously.

Take as many electives as you can handle that are aligned with your career. You will have specific classes you have to take to satisfy your major, but in many cases, you'll be offered a choice between two classes, both of which will satisfy a part of your degree. If you are able, take both choices because often they are both highly relevant to your career and will teach you a different aspect of the field. The more education and information you can get about your career while you're in college, the more prepared you'll be when you actually start working in it.

Join Career-Related Clubs and Volunteer for Career-Related Organizations and Causes

It will take a little time for you to get your feet under you when you first start college, but once you do, you'll discover there are dozens of clubs you can join and volunteer opportunities you can participate in, all on campus or very close to campus. Even if your high school had numerous club choices available to you, that number won't compare to what's available to you at college.

Start by joining one club that's relevant to your career path and add others as you have time. Keep your volunteering going strong by supporting organizations and causes that offer you experience in your field of choice. It's not about impressing college admissions officers anymore but rather about having a well-rounded resume and LinkedIn profile when you start applying for jobs in your industry.

Continue Working Part-Time to Build Your Resume

Working and going to college full-time isn't easy, but in addition to earning your own money, you want to continue getting real job experience, particularly if you can get it in a position that's relevant to your future career aspirations. Many colleges offer jobs in various departments, so you might be able to work in a position that supports your major. However, these jobs are hard to get, so don't limit yourself to what's available on campus.

We also want to reiterate that working in any part-time job at this juncture is going to give you valuable experience toward any career. Plus, it gives you an opportunity to refine your time-management skills by juggling both a job and class schedule. Employers like to see that you've successfully managed a busy life and were able to handle the pressure of having a job while going to school full-time.

Develop Your Resume

If you haven't already done so, now is the time to develop your resume in order to have it ready if internship or job opportunities arise. A resume is basically your introduction of yourself to a potential employer, so it needs to be polished and thorough. It's your first impression, and as the saying goes, you never get a second chance to make a good first impression.

Potential employers get dozens and sometimes hundreds of resumes and applications for open positions; you want to make sure your resume stands out. This may seem daunting since you're just starting out in your career, but it can be done. There are plenty of tips on how to create an eye-catching resume online, even without a lot of experience to fill it, so you'll want to research various resume designs and styles before committing to one. Additionally, you should seek out career-specific resume examples to tailor your resume to opportunities in your field of choice.

Most colleges and universities have a job center that can help you with your resume. They have experts available to give you advice and help you create a resume that will cut through all the noise to the hiring manager. You will also need a cover letter that intrigues the hiring manager enough to continue onto to your resume, and the job center can assist with that as well.

You will continue to add to and tweak your resume as you progress in your college experience. Your resume is something that will stay with you for a lifetime. For now, list all your experience in various jobs, clubs, volunteer activities, and education to ensure you have a robust resume that demonstrates your eagerness to learn and work in your desired career. Eventually, these early experiences will drop off your resume as you gain better and more relevant positions that will take their place.

Identify Possible Internship Opportunities

It's never too early to begin thinking about internship opportunities. Many companies these days want to see at least one career-related internship on your resume before they'll consider offering you a permanent position. Typically, college students intern during the summer between the spring and fall terms, so you can start to identify possible internship opportunities as early as your freshman year.

Even if you don't intern until the summer between your sophomore and junior year or later, you should be aware of the opportunities that are out there. Some of the best resources to help you find internship opportunities include:

- Campus bulletin boards and intranet department sites
- Local businesses in your desired field
- Online job boards and internship-specific boards such as:
  - Indeed
  - Monster
  - Glassdoor
  - Chegg.com
  - CollegeRecruiter.com

- o InternJobs.com
- o Internships.com

Remember that internships are often unpaid, so you will probably need to keep a part-time job while you intern, if possible. Depending on the hours your internship requires, you may need to adjust your part-time job availability to accommodate your internship, as this will be extremely valuable to your career.

Attend Career Fairs

You can also find excellent internship opportunities by attending career fairs. Remember the first time you attended job fairs during your career-planning journey? Your goal was to explore jobs and get an idea of what a person does in certain careers in order to narrow down your options. This time, you're attending job fairs to actually get hired for an internship or job. As such, your approach to these job fairs will be a little different than your preliminary visits.

To begin with, you'll need that resume you've been working on. Make at least a dozen copies and possibly more depending on how many companies you're interested in working for. If it's a specialty job fair that is geared toward your career, you may need 20 or more copies of your resume, even if you just want companies to keep it on file for future job or internship openings.

It's also very possible that you could interview with companies during your visit to a job fair. While some fairs might require appointments for interviews, others will allow companies to conduct interviews on the spot. So, to make sure you're prepared for that possibility, you'll want to practice interviewing before you arrive at the fair. Look up common interview questions and rehearse your answers to them. Put each question on a flashcard and shuffle them so you get used to answering them in any order.

If possible, have someone act in the role of the interviewer as you answer questions. Have them give you feedback on your responses, body language, and presentation (things like tone, volume, etc.). If you can't find someone to roleplay with you, consider recording yourself so that you can observe these things on your own and make adjustments to your responses accordingly. When you're practicing, dress up as if you're attending the real interview. This will allow you to get into the part and ensure your clothing doesn't distract from your answers. The day of your interview is not the time to realize your clothes don't fit right or are too casual for the event.

As mentioned earlier, at a job fair, you may be trying to land an interview on the spot. If so, you'll need to develop what is known as an "elevator pitch" that will get you in the door for a longer interview. It's meant to be short enough to deliver all the important parts of your experience, background, and education in a single elevator ride from the ground floor to an upper floor. As such, your pitch needs to be around a minute or less.

In your elevator pitch, include bullet points on yourself, such as your education, one or two relevant skills, a brief summary of any relevant experience, and a synopsis of your career aspirations. In this case, since you're looking for an internship, be sure to mention that as well. Try to tailor your elevator pitch to the job role you're looking for, if there is one, and to an internship in general if there isn't one.

Practice your pitch over and over again until you can deliver it with confidence and at an appropriate pace. It's tempting to speed through an elevator pitch, but if you've only focused on the most important parts of your education, experience, and aspirations, you have enough time to slow down and make sure your audience understands you. Follow up your elevator pitch by giving the representative your resume and asking them to consider you for a full interview.

Here's an example of an ideal elevator pitch for career fairs:

"I'm Lea, and I'm a sophomore at UCLA. I'm majoring in marketing with a goal of pursuing a career in brand management. I have worked part-time in retail for three years, where I continue to learn various marketing strategies, and I've participated in creating social media marketing campaigns for UCLA's alumni organization to raise funds for the school. This summer, I hope to have a marketing internship that will prepare me for my future in the field."

As you gain more experience in your field of choice, you can update your pitch with more details about your skills. Every time you complete an internship or learn a new skill at a job, consider adding it to your elevator pitch. Right now, your pitch will be fairly general in nature but will become more specific as you continue your journey.

Before you arrive at the career fair, you should know which companies will have representatives there. This will help you determine which ones you really want to visit and those that you will only visit if you have time. Create a plan to make the most of your time there, starting with the company you most want to see. This way, if you get an interview, you'll have plenty of time to complete it. The representatives for each company should be able to tell you if they're conducting interviews on the spot or if they will be scheduled at a later date. This will help you decide how much time to spend at each booth. For example, if company A isn't conducting on-site interviews, you can just drop off your resume and move on to company B, which is holding interviews that day.

You should also take the time to establish or update your LinkedIn profile. This is a professional social media platform that is becoming a critical pre-screening tool for prospective employers. They like to look at your profile in conjunction with your resume to make sure everything lines up and check if there is any additional information on your profile that's not on your resume.

The nice thing about LinkedIn is that you're not restricted to one or two pages like you are with a resume. Go ahead and list everything relevant or irrelevant to your desired career, including your part-time job experience, clubs, and volunteer work. It's the perfect place for you to go in depth on anything you don't have room for on a resume. Just be sure all content is professionally written and that you use an appropriate photograph for your profile photo.

On the day of the career fair, dress as if you're going to a job interview because essentially, you are. This means no jeans, shorts, tank tops, flip flops, sneakers, or other casualwear. Slacks, suits, dresses, ties, dress shoes, blouses, and other business attire will be expected by employers, and you want to put your best foot forward right from the start. Of course, if you aren't attending a job fair with traditional employers, you should dress according to the field's standards, but dressing up never hurts.

Mid- and Late Post-Secondary

Your sophomore, junior, and senior years in college are going to look quite similar to each other in terms of career planning. While you're going to continue taking classes that are increasingly specialized for your major and career, the bulk of your career-planning process will be centered on getting experience from internships and part-time jobs. Your courses will provide the appropriate curriculums to give you the knowledge you need to earn your degree, but it will be incumbent upon you to find those outside opportunities that will increase your experience level.

Essentially, you should continue maintaining your GPA at the level you need to graduate, participating in career-related clubs, volunteering with career-related organizations or causes, and working part-time to build your resume. In the summers between terms, you should be interning at companies to gain relevant skills and experience for your career. If possible, try to intern in different roles that allow you to experience various aspects of the field.

In your late junior or early senior year, you will have a few choices to make, including whether you're going to continue your education in a graduate program or you're going to apply for full-time jobs in your career field. This could be a more challenging decision than you think, especially if you know your ultimate job title and position is going to require additional education.

If you decide to attend graduate school, you'll want to repeat the steps outlined in the Mid– and Late High School sections, substituting graduate schools for post-secondary programs. You'll want to research your graduate school options. This includes noting enrollment requirements, fees, and other pertinent information; taking any required entrance exams (LSAT, GRE,

GMAT, MCAT, etc.); and following the application guidelines to the letter (deadlines, attachments, essays, etc.).

If you're going to work for a while before pursuing your graduate degree, or you don't intend to attend graduate school at all, you should begin applying for jobs in the spring semester of your senior year. The best way to do this is to follow the steps for finding an internship in the Early Post-Secondary section, except you'll search for jobs instead of internships.

In all instances, be sure to use your school's career or job center to help you transition from college to the workforce. This resource is invaluable and can really make a difference in the type of job you get once you've graduated. Your school wants you to succeed in whatever career you choose, so take advantage of the assistance you can get from the experts at the career center.

In rare cases, you might also discover at this time that you aren't as well-suited for the career you chose and planned for. If this is how you feel as your graduation is upon you, don't panic! People change careers all the time, and it's definitely possible for you to rework your future. You can follow an accelerated version of your initial career plan to help you choose another one, or you can get expert advice from a life coach. Either way, don't feel like you're stuck just because you spent a lot of time getting to where you are.

READY TO FLY!

By the time you're in the final year of your education plan, you will be ready to take the leap and enter the career of your choice. Of course, you will still have work to do to reach the level you ultimately want, but thanks to your comprehensive career plan, you'll have your foot in the door.

Having a plan is one of the best ways to reach any goal, and your career is one of the biggest goals you'll ever have. Don't leave this important part of your life up to chance. Start career planning now so that you can thrive in the future of your dreams.